The Day the Milk Spilled

The Day the Milk Spilled

... And 30 Other Bible-Based Meditations

Series # 5

Roger Ellsworth

Unless otherwise noted, Scripture quotations are taken from the New King James Version®. Copyright © 1982 by Thomas Nelson. Used by permission. All rights reserved.

Copyright © 2018, Roger Ellsworth

All rights reserved. No part of this book may be reproduced, scanned, or distributed in any printed or electronic form without permission.

First Edition: 2018

ISBN: 978-0-9965168-6-0

20180220LSI

Great Writing Publications
www.greatwriting.org
Taylors, SC

www.greatwriting.org

Purpose

My Coffee Cup Meditations are short, easy-to-read, engagingly presented devotions based on the Bible, the Word of God. Each reading takes a single idea or theme and develops it in a thought-provoking way so that you are inspired to consider the greatness of God, the relevance of the good news of the life, death, resurrection, and coming-again of Jesus, and are better equipped for life in this world and well prepared for the world to come.

www.mycoffeecupmeditations.com

https://www.facebook.com/MyCoffeeCupMeditations/

Dedication

Dedicated to my friend from youth,
Sandy Mullen

About This Book

This book is the result of the labors Roger Ellsworth and the thought he has given to various passages of Scripture over the years. You may read more about Roger on page 141.

We hope you will enjoy these Bible-based meditations. We would love to hear from you, so please send us a note to tell us what you think—which ones you liked most, and how they made a difference in your life or in the life of a family member, friend, or work associate. To reach us online, go to
www.mycoffeecupmeditations.com/contact

MY COFFEE-CUP MEDITATIONS

Table of Contents

1 The Day the Milk Spilled 16
2 What about Jacob Eames? 20
3 The Greater Story 24
4 Get It Together, Dagwood! 28
5 The Man on His Way to the River 32
6 The Hymn Born in a Jelly Jar 36
7 The Names and the Name in the Bible 40
8 Flipped into Eternity 44
9 The Family of Faith 48
10 First in Three Ways 52
11 The Most Surprising Members of the Family (1) 56
12 The Most Surprising Members of the Family (2) 60
13 The Ax and the Cross 64
14 The Fear of a Churchman 68
15 The Extraordinary 72
16 The Best Christmas Ever 76
17 When Matthew Henry Was Robbed 80
18 Christ Above All Else 84
19 Skunks and Honey Buns 88
20 A Wasted Sheet of Paper 92
21 Christians Neglecting Salvation 96
22 The Red Horse in the Myrtle Grove 100
23 Propitiation and Diapers 104
24 A Man in a Vise (1) 108
25 A Man in a Vise (2) 112

26 Focusing Faith (1) 116
27 Focusing Faith (2) 120
28 Faith Keeps in Mind the Big Picture (1) 124
29 Faith Keeps in Mind the Hidden and Final Pictures (2) 128
30 Third Verses Only 132
31 Sad Sadducees! 136

About the Author 141
The Series 142

The App

www.mycoffeecupmeditations.com

Be sure you get the app!

-1-

From God's Word, the Bible...

Though the fig tree may not blossom,
Nor fruit be on the vines;
Though the labor of the olive may fail,
And the fields yield no food;
Though the flock may be cut off from the fold,
And there be no herd in the stalls —
Yet I will rejoice in the LORD,
I will joy in the God of my salvation.

Habakkuk 3:17-18

The Day the Milk Spilled

"Don't cry over spilled milk." How many times have we heard that one? It's a good saying. It means there's no point in fretting and stewing over things that can't be changed.

I can't tell you how this saying came about. I wouldn't be surprised if the first person to say it was a mother whose child spilled his milk and burst into tears. But that's just a guess.

I do recall a day when I saw someone crying over spilled milk. The someone wasn't a child. It was my dad. And the milk wasn't the small amount in a glass. It was a lot of milk.

For years my parents tried to scratch a living out of a hardscrabble little farm near Mulberry Grove, Illinois. There wasn't much money to be made from farming in those days, at least not from farming on our scale.

My parents would make some money when the crops were harvested, but that was annual income. As far as the vital weekly income was concerned, they had to depend on their hens and their cows for what they called the "egg money" and the "milk money."

They received the "egg money" when they sold their graded and boxed eggs to a merchant in Mulberry. And they received their "milk money" when a check arrived in the mail for the milk that was transported by truck from our little farm to town.

Our farm was isolated. It was a couple of miles from what my parents called the hard road. So there was a dirt road that extended from the hard road to our house and barn. The dirt road became a mud road when there was a lot of rain. When the road turned to mud, it was impossible for the milk truck to pick up our milk. On such days it was necessary for us to take the ten-gallon milk cans by tractor and trailer to the truck at the end of the hard road.

We were in this process one rainy day when disaster struck. The trailer hitch suddenly came loose and the trailer "tongue" flew up, sending the milk cans crashing into the mud. It was a strange sight, seeing that white milk cascading over the brown mud.

My dad wasn't a crier. As far as I can remember, I saw him cry on only one occasion—the day the milk spilled.

There was nothing to do except rehitch the trailer, pick up the empty milk cans, turn the tractor around, and make our way back down the muddy road, wondering all the way how we would make it without "the milk money."

Tears still well up when I think about it.

The milk in the mud left an unforgettable image in my mind, but it wasn't the only thing. When it was time for our next meal, we all bowed our heads as my father gave thanks for our food. And the next Sunday we were all in our usual places at church. The giving of thanks before eating and the going to church also etched indelible images in my mind.

Through their praying and churchgoing, my parents taught me that we don't trust and serve God because we think in doing so we will purchase for ourselves a trouble-free life. We trust and serve God because He is God. We don't trust Him to do what we want done, but rather to do as He has promised to do. And He has never promised to keep the milk out of the mud.

The prophet Habakkuk could imagine a time when the fig tree would not blossom, the vines and olive trees would not produce, the fields would be barren, and there would be no livestock. In other words, he could imagine a time when the milk would be in the mud. So what does he say about such a time? Does he say that will be the time to stop loving and trusting God? Not at all! He rather says:

> *Yet I will rejoice in the LORD,*
> *I will joy in the God of my salvation.*

If we want to rejoice, we must not look to the milk in the mud but rather to the Lord Jesus Christ on the cross. There He purchased salvation for sinners so they can join Him in heaven where there will be no more milk in the mud and no more tears (Rev. 21:4).

-2-

From God's Word, the Bible...

*He who believes in the Son has everlasting life; and he who does
not believe the Son shall not see life,
but the wrath of God abides on him.*

John 3:36

What about Jacob Eames?

They became very close friends when they were students at Providence College (later to be named Brown University)—Adoniram Judson and Jacob Eames.

Judson was brought up by godly parents. His father, after whom he was named, was a pastor. But when he went to college—as so often seems to be the case—the young Judson turned against the faith of his parents. One of the main reasons was his friend Jacob Eames. Jacob rejected the Bible and the God of the Bible. He was so intelligent and witty! And Adoniram was mesmerized—so much so that he joined Jacob in repudiating the Christian faith.

Knowing his new views would devastate his parents, Adoniram kept them to himself for a while. When he told his parents he had decided to travel, they tried to dissuade him. In the heat of disagreeing, Adoniram told his father that he no longer believed the Bible was the Word of God or Jesus was the Son of God.

Adoniram made his way to New York City with the hope of finding a career in the theater. It was not to be. Disappointed and dejected, he left the city. He stopped to spend the night in a village inn. It wasn't a restful night. A man in the next room was critically ill. As he heard the sick man groaning through the night, Adoniram was torn. On one hand, he wondered if this man was ready to die, and if he, Adoniram, was ready. On the other hand, he could imagine what his friend Jacob Eames would say to him if he were there with him: "Are you, the valedictorian of Brown University, going to allow yourself to be carried away by religious superstition?"

The next morning Adoniram asked the innkeeper about the man in the adjoining room. "He is dead," answered the innkeeper.

"Do you know who he was?" asked Adoniram.

The response was stunning: "Oh yes, a young man from the college in Providence. Eames, Jacob Eames."

That news caused Adoniram's mind to whirl. He couldn't get the word "Lost" out of his head.

> Lost. In death, Jacob Eames was lost—utterly, irrevocably lost. Lost to his friends, to the world, to the future. Lost as a puff of smoke is lost in the infinity of air. If Eames' own views were true, neither his life nor his death had any meaning. . . . But suppose Eames had been mistaken? Suppose the Scriptures were literally true and a personal God real? Then Jacob Eames was already lost in a most desperate sense. For already, this moment, Eames knew his error—too late for repentance. . . any chance of remedy, of going back, of correcting, lost, eternally lost.[1]

---

[1] (Courtney Anderson, *To the Golden Shore: The Life of Adoniram Judson*).

Realizing that his friend's haughty skepticism was no defense in the face of death, Adoniram turned to the gospel of Christ that he had so confidently repudiated. Eames' death caused Adoniram to see this: proud intellectualism can be a very delectable morsel, but it loses its appeal when served on the plate of death.

Adoniram Judson would go on to a life of serving that gospel as a missionary in Burma and to a life of incredible suffering for that gospel. Unlike his friend Jacob Eames, Adoniram would die believing that gospel and drawing comfort from it.

The gospel of Jesus Christ served as a dividing line for Adoniram Judson and Jacob Eames. Adoniram was on one side of it, and Eames on the other. It is still dividing. Each and every one of us is either on the Jacob Eames side of the gospel or on the Adoniram side. The former is the side of haughty, disdainful rejection; the latter the side of humble acceptance. The Eames side is that of dying without hope; the Adoniram side makes dying nothing more than falling asleep in the arms of the Lord.

On which side are you? If you are on the Eames side, you don't have to remain there. You can be on the Adoniram side by repenting of your sins and trusting in the Lord Jesus.

Many maintain that they are on neither side. They insist that they are neutral. But Jesus said: "He who is not with Me is against Me, and he who does not gather with Me scatters abroad" (Matt. 12:30). Are you with Him or against Him?

-3-

From God's Word, the Bible...

For we do not preach ourselves, but Christ Jesus the Lord, and ourselves your bondservants for Jesus' sake.

2 Corinthians 4:5

The Greater Story

April of 1846 found Adoniram Judson, missionary to Burma, back in America for the first time since his departure in 1812. One of those April days found him in Hamilton, New York, where he addressed a congregation of eager hearers. The building was packed. Due to an ongoing problem with his throat, Adoniram spoke for only fifteen minutes about the Lord Jesus Christ. His fiancée, Emily Chubbock, said the message was about what Christ "has done for us, and what we owe to him." Emily characterized the message as one of "singular simplicity" and "touching pathos."

But there was a problem. Both Adoniram and Emily sensed that his words had not been well received. Emily noted: "… it was evident, even to the most unobservant eye, that most of the listeners were disappointed."

After the service, she learned the reason. The people had come expecting Judson to tell the exciting story of his time in Burma. When Emily related this to Adoniram, he responded that there is nothing better to tell than "the wondrous story of Jesus' dying love."

Adoniram Judson certainly had many interesting stories to tell about his missionary service in Burma. He could have talked about frightening voyages, frustrating delays, life-threatening diseases, heart-wrenching imprisonment, and death. Yes, he knew all about death, having lost two wives and six children in the first thirty-three years of his time in Burma.

But to him the story of his service in Burma could not begin to compare with the story of Jesus.

There are things to learn from Adoniram's experience in Hamilton, New York. One thing is that it is possible to keep the wonder of salvation, no matter how long we have been saved and no matter how many difficulties we have encountered. Adoniram had kept it, and so should we. But the flipside is true also. It's possible to lose the wonder of salvation. I'm not talking about losing salvation itself, but rather losing the sense of amazement over it. Many people in Adoniram's congregation, if not most, had apparently lost that sense of amazement.

The author of Hebrews bemoaned the fact that he had so much of a wondrous nature to share with his readers, but they had become "dull of hearing" (Heb. 5:11).

How do we "stack up" in the wonderment business? Are we in Adoniram's stack or that of his hearers?

Doesn't the current tendency of pastors and churches to embrace an entertainment mentality tell us that the saving work of Jesus doesn't thrill us? Doesn't the tendency of preachers to pitch their preaching toward coping with the challenges of life tell us that they're not as thrilled about the Lord Jesus as they should be? If we are going to preach the Bible, we must preach the Lord Jesus because He is the subject of the Bible.

Adoniram and Emily were married on June 2, 1846. On July 11, they set sail for Burma, arriving there in late November. But their time there would be brief. Adoniram became so gravely ill that it was decided that he must leave. He died on board the *Aristide Marie* that was carrying him away on April 12, 1850. A coffin was constructed for him, and in the darkness of the night, it was released into the darkness of the ocean to await the day that the sea will give up the dead who are in it (Rev. 20:13).

How are we to explain Adoniram Judson? How are we to explain his remarkable accomplishments and his ability to absorb suffering? We could say that by nature he possessed unusual strength of character, and we would be correct. But I think if Adoniram were asked to explain himself, he might very well do so in terms of the message he preached in Hamilton, New York—the message of what Christ has done for His people and what they owe Him. Adoniram would, I think, tell his story in terms of the far greater story, the story of Jesus. He loved that story, and he would urge us to love it as well.

> *Tell me the story of Jesus,*
> *Write on my heart every word.*
> *Tell me the story most precious,*
> *Sweetest that ever was heard.*
> (Fanny J. Crosby)

−4−

From God's Word, the Bible...

Now the days of David drew near that he should die, and he charged Solomon his son, saying: "I go the way of all the earth; be strong, therefore, and prove yourself a man. And keep the charge of the LORD your God: to walk in His ways, to keep His statutes, His commandments, His judgments, and His testimonies, as it is written in the Law of Moses, that you may prosper in all that you do and wherever you turn . . ."

1 Kings 2:1-3

Get It Together, Dagwood!

I have something to confess. I quit reading the comic strip "Blondie" years ago. I don't have anything against Blondie herself, you understand. It's her husband, Dagwood Bumstead, who drives me crazy.

Dagwood is almost everything that a man should not be. Call him the "Anti-Man." He's lazy, shiftless, and irresponsible. He's always running late, much to the chagrin of his fellow carpoolers. And when he is at work, he's always goofing off. It's always been amazing to me that his boss, Mr. Dithers, doesn't fire him. Maybe Mr. Dithers wouldn't dither so much if he didn't have Dagwood around.

When he is at home, Dagwood eats too much, sleeps too much, and quarrels with his neighbor Herb too much.

Dagwood isn't all bad. He is a faithful husband, but it's easy to see that he is such an exasperating fellow that Blondie and even his dog, Daisy, find it hard to put up with him.

So when it comes to comic strips, give me "Garfield" any day. What's that? You're saying Garfield is much like Dagwood—eating too much and sleeping too much? I admit it, Garfield is much like Dagwood, but there's a huge difference. Garfield is a cat. Dagwood is a man.

Yes, yes, I know Dagwood is a cartoon character. He exists to give us a chuckle or two. He is intended to lighten our load a bit as we journey along life's way. If he were a disciplined, responsible fellow, there wouldn't be anything to laugh about. We are not meant to take poor Dagwood seriously.

I agree. Although, I don't read "Blondie," it's all right with me if you do. Read it as much as you want and chuckle over Dagwood's follies and antics as much as you want, but, if you are a man, don't be like Dagwood. Being a man is serious business. So very much hinges on men being men— marriages, families, careers, churches, and even all of society. Disciplined, responsible living isn't funny, but it is essential.

Several years ago, "real men" jokes were common. One went like this: How many real men does it take to change a light bulb? None. Real men aren't afraid of the dark.

I suggest being real men means, in part, doing what we have contracted to do, when we're supposed to do it, and in the way it's supposed to be done.

If we want to know what it is to be a real man, we only have to look to the greatest man who ever lived. That would be the Lord Jesus Christ. He did what He contracted to do (the work of providing salvation for sinners), at the time He was supposed to do it (the time God the Father had appointed, the fullness of time—Gal. 4:4), and in the way He was supposed to do it (not sullenly and grudgingly but gladly and willingly).

He, the Second Person of the Trinity, willingly took our

humanity. As a man, He perfectly obeyed the laws of God. He lived the life that we have failed to live. Then He went to the cross to die the death we deserve to die for our sins, receiving the wrath of God in our place.

We might say that the greatest of all men (Jesus) did the greatest of all work (salvation).

For men to be real men, they must look to Jesus. They must receive the salvation that He came to provide by repenting of their sins and by placing their faith in Him. After that, they must make it their business to seek every day to think as He would think, speak as He would speak, and do as He would do with these words echoing in their minds:

> *Ye that are men now serve Him*
> *Against unnumbered foes;*
> *Let courage rise with danger,*
> *And strength to strength oppose.*
> (George Duffield, Jr.)

I can tell you this much—when my sons were growing up, I never suggested that they look to Dagwood Bumstead as a role model. My word to them was "Look to Jesus" (Heb. 12:2).

-5-

From God's Word, the Bible...

I charge you therefore before God and the Lord Jesus Christ, who will judge the living and the dead at His appearing and His kingdom: Preach the word! Be ready in season and out of season. Convince, rebuke, exhort, with all longsuffering and teaching.

2 Timothy 4:1-2

The Man on His Way to the River

Although Martyn Lloyd-Jones died many years ago, on March 1, 1981, he is still my favorite preacher. My wife and I hold him in such high esteem that we named our second son after him—Martyn Ellsworth. Marty is also a preacher, and in my estimation one of the best to be found.

Are you familiar with Lloyd-Jones? Although he had a promising career in medicine before him, Lloyd-Jones went into the gospel ministry. After a noteworthy pastorate in Wales, Lloyd-Jones became first the co-pastor and then the pastor of Westminster Chapel in London. He served from 1939 to 1945 in the former role and from 1945 to 1968 in the latter.

One of my favorite Lloyd-Jones stories has to do with a man who was on his way one Sunday evening to the River Thames. He was going to end his miserable life by throwing himself into those dark, chilly waters. Years before, the man had come to faith in Christ, but he had strayed far from God.

As the poor fellow came to Westminster Bridge, he heard the chimes of Big Ben striking. He realized it was time for Lloyd-Jones to start his sermon. He decided that before ending his life he would walk the short distance to the church and listen. As he sat down, he heard Lloyd-Jones say: "God have mercy on the backslider."

The man immediately turned back to God and went on to live his remaining years as a faithful servant of the Lord Jesus.

I've thought a lot about this man over the years. Many times I've prayed this prayer as I've stood to preach: "Lord, help me to remember the man on his way to the river."

That was the way I reminded myself of the importance of what I was about to do. It reminded me that the preacher can never be sure who is in his audience and what needs may be present among those who hear him. So he must preach with passion and urgency.

The pastor and church members may say: "There's no man on his way to the river who needs to get into our church."

But there are men and women and boys and girls on their way to eternity—and not just some of them, but all of them. The sad truth is that many church services seem to take place on the assumption that no lost person could possibly be there.

We need to think as Richard Baxter thought: "I preach as a dying man to dying men and as never sure to preach again."

Imagine with me. It's late on Sunday afternoon, and Mr. Eternity-Bound Man is sitting in his living room watching television. Suddenly, there is breaking news. A prominent person has died very unexpectedly. Mr. Eternity-Bound hasn't thought about dying for a long time, but he thinks about it now. He, too, must die. What then? He becomes so disturbed about his soul that he decides to go to church.

He may not realize it, but he is immediately facing some very large problems. One is that it might be very difficult for him to locate a church that is open on Sunday evenings. Another is that in those churches that are open, he might find it very hard to find a church where there is preaching. Yet another problem is that if there were preaching, it might not include anything about what eternity-bound people must do to be saved. Yet another is that if he were to hear such a sermon, it could be delivered in a very dispassionate way.

Yes, I know God doesn't need Sunday evening services and sermons to save people, but I also know that the God who could work *without us* has chosen to work *through us*. The same God who ordains certain ends also ordains means to attain those ends. If God has chosen the salvation of sinners as His end, we can rest assured that He has also chosen prayer, preaching, witnessing, giving, and other means to reach that end. Let's be using those means and trusting the Lord to make them effective.

Who knows? We might be used by God to help a man on his way to the river. It's exciting to know that we can be instruments of His grace to point such a person to the safety that can be found in the wonderful person and perfect work of the Savior. The Lord Jesus now calls and commands all people to turn to Him in repentance and faith, to experience the new birth, and be assured of sins forgiven and a glorious home forever in heaven.

-6-

From God's Word, the Bible...

*They shall see His face, and His
name shall be on their foreheads.*

Revelation 22:4

The Hymn Born in a Jelly Jar

Grant Colfax Tullar liked jelly, and all of his friends knew he liked jelly. So when he sat down to eat with some of them, it was no surprise that they handed to him the almost-empty jelly jar.

"This is all for me?" Grant asked. When his friends assured him that it was, he repeated: "All for me!"

In a flash of inspiration, he rose from the table, went to the piano, and composed a hymn that began:

> *All for me, the Savior suffered,*
> *All for me, He bled and died.*

When the mail arrived the next morning in his New Jersey home, Grant found a poem from Carrie Breck, who lived in Portland, Oregon. He soon realized that the words of this poem were an ideal match for the music that he had written the previous evening.

So an almost-empty jelly jar led to *All for Me*, and the music for *All for Me* led to this hymn:

> *Face to face with Christ my Savior,*
> *Face to face what will it be,*
> *When with rapture I behold Him,*
> *Jesus Christ who died for me.*
> *Face to face I shall behold Him,*
> *Far beyond the starry sky;*
> *Face to face in all His glory,*
> *I shall see Him by and by.*

We can't say what Grant Tullar did with his original lyrics. Perhaps he stored them away in an empty jelly jar! That's not to say there was something wrong with them. There wasn't. It was rather a matter of him recognizing that Carrie's poem more perfectly agreed with the music he had composed.

Carrie Breck, a busy housewife and mother (she and her husband had five daughters), often wrote poems as she was going about her daily tasks. *Face to Face* is the best known of the 2,000 poems she wrote.

Carrie's poem and Grant's music combined to give us a hymn that has brought blessing and encouragement to the multitudes who have read it and sung it since 1898.

It is a hymn that blends calm, settled assurance with joyful expectancy and breathless wonder.

The calm, settled assurance is found in the word "shall," which appears four times. It's not a word that allows for uncertainty.

The joyful expectancy is found in this phrase: "When with rapture I behold Him." "Rapture" conveys ecstasy, elation, and euphoria. It's also found in the phrase "O, blissful moment." "Blissful" conveys complete happiness.

Then there's the phrase "What rejoicing in His presence."

The breathless wonder comes out in the phrase "Face to face, what will it be." With those words, Carrie Breck is saying to us: "Stop and think for a moment what it will be like to be face to face with the Lord Jesus."

One wonders where the people of the world find wonder. Where do they find something that is so much greater than themselves that they can only stand in awe? Is it something that is really quite small such as a sporting event? Is that it? Christians find it in the One who came from glory to take them to glory. What vast distances are involved in that! Jesus came all the way from heaven's glory to the depths of our sin to take us from those depths to heaven's glory. Who can measure the gap between the throne from which He came to the cross on which He died?

It's Jesus' death on the cross that gives Christians the assurance that they will meet Him face to face. Why was He on that cross? It was to receive the penalty that we deserve for our sins. Oh, the depths into which He descended on the cross—the depths of the wrath of God in the place of sinners! If He would do that part of redemption's work for us, we should never doubt that He will do the rest of it as well. And the rest of it is meeting Him face to face. Carrie Breck found in that word "Redeemer" all she needed to assure her of that face-to-face meeting.

> *Face to face! O blissful moment!*
> *Face to face to see and know;*
> *Face to face with my Redeemer,*
> *Jesus Christ who loves me so.*

-7-

From God's Word, the Bible...

And she will bring forth a Son, and you shall call His name Jesus, for He will save His people from their sins.

Matthew 1:21

The Names and the Name in the Bible

Through the years I have perpetrated on my grandchildren, much to their dismay, a bit of foolishness that goes like this:

> *I've never seen a purple cow,*
> *I hope I never see one.*
> *But I can tell you anyhow,*
> *I'd rather see one than be one.*

When it comes to multi-syllabic Bible names, I say: "I'd rather see it than be it." In other words, I'm glad my parents didn't give me one of those names.

Every preacher knows what it is to tremble at the thought of publicly reading passages with hard-to-pronounce names. I have always told myself to pronounce those challenging names any way I choose because none of the listeners will have the slightest idea what the correct pronunciation is. On the reading of those gnarled Bible names, my advice to intimidated preachers has always been this: "Just act like you know what you're doing, and no one will be the wiser."

That rule, of course, has its limits. It won't work if the preacher, as one preacher did, pronounces Nebuchadnezzar as "Nee-buck-a-neezer."

If anyone does challenge one of my pronunciations, I'm ready to ask: "And how would you pronounce it?"

So while I greatly prefer Og, Huz and Buz (twin brothers), and Gob (a place), I don't mind taking a run at Ashurbanipal, Lo-Ruhamah, Magor-Missabib, Misrephoth-Maim, Chushanrishathaim, Zaphnathpaaneah, Tilgathpilneser, Berodachbaladan, Epaphroditus, and, my personal favorite, Maher-Shalal-Hash-Baz. My word to all of them is this: "Take your best shot. You're not going to scare me." You could just call me "The Master of the Monikers."

In Proverbs 22:1, Solomon says:

A good name is to be chosen rather than great riches ....

In Ecclesiastes 7:1, he adds:

A good name is better than precious ointment...

What is a good name? It's not one that is easy to pronounce. One can have an easily pronounced name and not have a good name. Conversely, one can have a name that is filled with twists and turns, and yet it is a good name.

A good name is one that is associated with good things. It's a name that causes people to think of those traits we most admire—honesty, decency, morality, kindness, fairness, truthfulness, and dependability.

When we hear someone's name, certain qualities almost

invariably leap to mind. What qualities come to mind when someone hears your name? We should all try to live in such a way that the mere mention of our names causes people to think of the virtues Paul mentioned in his letter to the Philippians: "Finally, brethren, whatever things are true, whatever things are noble, whatever things are just, whatever things are lovely, whatever things are of good report, if there is any virtue and if there is anything praiseworthy—meditate on these things" (Phil. 4:8).

A good name is a wonderful thing. Solomon says it is better to have it than to be rich. It should be our goal to so live that others consider us to be good.

But we must also have a higher goal, that is, to have God consider us to be good. We can indeed appear good to others and yet not appear good to God. When He was addressed as "Good Teacher," Jesus responded: "No one is good but One, that is, God" (Mark 10:18). No, Jesus wasn't saying He wasn't good. Quite the opposite! He was saying that He was God!

The greatest of all questions is this: How can a perfectly good God ever consider us to be good when He is already on record as saying no one is good? (See Ps. 14:1-3; 53:1-3; Eccl. 7:20; Rom. 10:10.)

The answer lies in Jesus. He lived the perfectly good life that God demands, and that good life He lived is credited to us when we repent of our sins and trust in Him as our Lord and Savior.

The long and short of it is this—it's okay to stumble over the difficult names of the Bible, but make sure you understand that the greatest of all names is Jesus (Phil. 2:5-11).

-8-

From God's Word, the Bible...

Do not labor for the food which perishes, but for the food which endures to everlasting life, which the Son of Man will give you, because God the Father has set His seal on Him.

John 6:27

Flipped into Eternity

My brother-in-law, John, owned a farm next to one owned by Al. One day John and my dad were engaged in conversation as they stood in the shade of one of John's trees. They happened to see Al speeding across his pasture as fast as his tractor could take him. Suddenly the front wheels of that Allis Chalmers tractor hit something, causing it to flip. Hoping to find that Al had been thrown clear and was uninjured, John and my dad ran to the spot. There was nothing they could do. Al was already dead with the steering wheel of his tractor planted firmly on his chest.

One of the many things I admired about my dad was his concern for the souls of others. He had been concerned for a long time about Al and had witnessed to him on several occasions. I remember being with him on one of those occasions. Al's response ran along these lines: "I like you, and I like having you as one of my neighbors, but I'm not interested in your religion."

I don't know for sure what Al's spiritual condition was

when he went out into eternity. I've always nurtured the hope that he had on that very day turned to Christ and, seeing my dad from afar, was hurrying to tell him the good news. That's what I hope, but I'm not sure. I know Al heard enough of the gospel from my dad that he could have been saved.

I'm sure some are saved very late in life, so much so that with their last breath they pray for mercy. I've always been thankful for the account of the last-minute conversion of one of the two thieves crucified alongside Jesus (Luke 23:42-43). And I'm thankful for the insightful comment of J.C. Ryle about those two thieves: "One thief was saved that no sinner might despair, but only one, that no sinner might presume."

But I do know this—Al went out into eternity. And so shall we all. How very certain it is! How little most seem to think about!

I can tell you this—eternity was constantly on the mind of the Lord Jesus Christ. And the Lord Jesus knows all there is to know about the eternal realm since He came from there to this world.

People these days like to believe that eternity is the same for everyone, but Jesus, the expert on the matter, says it is not so. He tells us that there are two parts to the eternal realm. One of those two parts He somberly labeled as "destruction." The other part He called "life" (Matt. 7:13-14).

We are all, without exception, going to one of those two parts. We are all either going to experience the destruction or the life.

And what is it that determines into which of the two realms we shall go? Is it a matter of doing a few good things here and there as we travel through life? Jesus, the expert, emphatically ruled that out (Matt. 7:21-23). He rather says in that best-loved of all Scripture verses, John 3:16, that only those who believe in Him have "everlasting life." Those who refuse to believe in Him will, to use Jesus' own word, "perish."

Jesus made it very plain in John 6:47: "Most assuredly, I say to you, he who believes in Me has everlasting life."

If we want to have the life, we must have the life-giver, Jesus (John 3:36; 1 John 5:11-12). It's as simple as that.

If you don't possess that life, consider the words of the Apostle Paul to the Philippian jailer: "Believe on the Lord Jesus Christ, and you will be saved ..." (Acts 16:31).

But be careful that you don't let that word "believe" make you think it is enough to merely have intellectual knowledge of Jesus. It is not enough. You must commit yourself to Christ, resting fully on what He did for sinners, as your only hope to enter into eternal life.

If you have believed in Christ, rejoice! Eternal destruction is forever behind you! Eternal life is gloriously before you!

Al's death taught me that we can be out in eternity in an instant. Let's be sure we're ready.

Are you ready?

-9-

From God's Word, the Bible...

Therefore we also, since we are surrounded by so great a cloud of witnesses, let us lay aside every weight, and the sin which so easily ensnares us, and let us run with endurance the race that is set before us, looking unto Jesus, the author and finisher of our faith, who for the joy that was set before Him endured the cross, despising the shame, and has sat down at the right hand of the throne of God.

Hebrews 12:1-2

The Family of Faith

Families are known for their gatherings. Birthday celebrations, Thanksgiving Day, and the Christmas season bring families together. Almost always, every family gathering is incomplete. Someone is missing.

Every Christian belongs to a family—the family of faith. The family of faith has never been together on this earth. It is after all a very, very old family—centuries and centuries old. But a time is coming when the family will finally be gathered together in one place—heaven.

In my many years as a pastor, I have had to answer one question about heaven more frequently than any other. What would you suppose that question to be? It is, much to my amazement, this: Will heaven be boring?

I've always responded to that with a question of my own: Why would you think that?

The answers I've gotten to that question usually stem from a fundamental misconception about heaven, namely, it will consist of shadowy figures floating around in the sky with harps in their hands and halos around their heads.

That, of course, is not heaven. Heaven in its final form is God's people living on a new earth in new bodies (Rev. 21:1-22:5).

Heaven will be endlessly fascinating. No one will ever be bored there. The main part of the fascination of heaven will be the Lord Jesus Christ. The sight of our Lord in glory has sometimes been called "the beatific vision," that is, "the happy-making sight." Every time we see the Lord Jesus in heaven's glory, we will rejoice with "joy inexpressible and full of glory" (1 Peter 1:8).

I'm convinced that another part of the fascination of heaven will be conversations with all of those family members. Imagine it! Sitting down to talk with Abraham, Moses, David, Elijah, Isaiah, Jeremiah, and Paul! And imagine conversing with Martin Luther, Charles Spurgeon, Jonathan Edwards, George Whitefield, and John and Charles Wesley. And let's not forget the women of faith we find in the Bible: Eve, Sarah, Ruth, Esther, Elizabeth, Mary, Anna, and Priscilla. Then there are those wonderful women of faith since the biblical era: Susannah Wesley, Fanny J. Crosby, Frances Havergal, Gladys Aylward, and Elizabeth Elliott, to only name a few.

There will be so much to discuss and so many questions to be asked and answered. But one question will never be asked in heaven. No one will ever ask anyone else how he or she got to heaven because everyone in heaven will know how everyone else got there. All will be there through faith in the redeeming work of Jesus Christ. So the Christian family is the family of faith. Through faith in the redeeming work of Jesus Christ, we are children of God and brothers and sisters in Christ. The family of faith is the family of God, and the family of God is the family of faith.

Another thing that will never be heard in heaven is people taking credit for their faith because they all will know very well that faith was itself the gift of God (Eph. 2:8-9; Phil. 1:29).

In these days of sloppy sentimentalism, most people seem to have the notion that we are all automatically part of the family of God. We are part of it, they say, merely by virtue of being born into this world. But that is not so. The Bible is clear. Being born once (physically) does not qualify us for heaven. We have to have a second birth, one that comes from above and creates within us the faith that lays hold of Christ (John 3:1-16).

Assuming that it is impossible for them to miss heaven, multitudes will in fact miss heaven. One of the main things that keep people from going to heaven is assuming that they are going there without faith in Christ. Those who do have that faith can gladly sing as their own the words of Bill Gaither:

From the door of an orphanage to the house of the King,
No longer an outcast, a new song I sing;
From rags unto riches, from the weak to the strong,
I'm not worthy to be here, but PRAISE GOD! *I belong!*

I'm so glad I'm a part of the Family of God.
I've been washed in the fountain, cleansed by His Blood!
Joint heirs with Jesus as we travel this sod,
For I'm part of the family,
The Family of God. [2]

---

[2] https://www.musixmatch.com/lyrics/Bill-Gaither-3/The-Family-of-God

-10-

From God's Word, the Bible...

*So God created man in His own image; in the image of God He created him; male and female He created them.
Then God blessed them, and God said to them, "Be fruitful and multiply; fill the earth and subdue it; have dominion over the fish of the sea, over the birds of the air, and over every living thing that moves on the earth."*

Genesis 1:27-28

First in Three Ways

The first members of the family of faith were Adam and Eve, but to say that is to get ahead of ourselves.

We must begin by saying Adam and Eve were *first on earth*. Adam was the first man to ever live, and Eve was the first woman to ever live. They were created by God. Adam was made from the dust of the earth, and Eve was taken from Adam's side.

Are we to actually believe these things? Yes, we most certainly are. The Lord Jesus believed that Adam and Eve were the first people (Matt. 19:4-6). He would be the One to know because He was the One who actually did the creating (Col. 1:16).

If we call Jesus "Lord" (and every Christian does), we are not at liberty to dispute what He says.

Adam and Eve were made by God and for God. They were made in His image and were made to live for His glory.

One way we bring glory to God is by obeying Him. In this way, we honor Him as our Creator and as our Sovereign.

God gave Adam and Eve one command to obey—not fifty or a hundred or a thousand—just one! They were not to eat of the tree of knowledge of good and evil.

Such a simple command! But Adam and Eve failed to obey it. So in addition to being the first people on earth, they were also the *first in sin*.

Yes, the devil, masquerading as a serpent, led Eve into sin, and Eve led Adam into sin. But Adam and Eve had no one to blame but themselves.

It was the greatest catastrophe of all time. No disaster that has happened since can compare to it. The fact that Adam and Eve plunged themselves into sin was only part of it. God had constituted Adam as the representative head of the whole human race. So his sin means we are all born into this world as sinners (Rom. 5:12-19). Like Adam, we are all made to live for the glory of God, but we all fail to do so (Rom. 3:23).

Sin is refusing to bring glory to God by refusing to conform to His laws. We are all called to be law-keepers, but, alas, we are all law-breakers.

Adam and Eve knew immediately that things were different because of their sin. They knew that they had fractured their fellowship with God, had alienated themselves from Him, and were deserving only of His judgment. The fact that they made aprons for themselves tells us that they knew that they were no longer fit to stand in His presence.

God could have left them to experience the horrible results of the sin that they had chosen, but He made Adam and Eve *first in saving grace*. He sought them out. He promised to send One who would make atonement for their sins (Gen. 3:15) and for the sins of all who would believe in Him. That one, of course, was the Lord Jesus Christ. God also threw away the worthless aprons they had made for themselves and made for them coats of animal skins. By slaying those animals, God pointed Adam and Eve ahead to the blood that Jesus would shed for their sins. That blood represented life poured out in death. In shedding His blood on the cross, Jesus poured out His life as He experienced not just physical death but also the eternal death that we deserve for our sins.

How the grace of God shined that day in Eden! The gospel was proclaimed there. God Himself was the preacher, Christ's atoning death was the subject, and Adam and Eve the audience. That day God called Adam and Eve to believe in the coming Christ, and believe they did. So they were first on earth, first in sin, and, thank God, first in faith.

Because of God's grace, Adam and Eve went to heaven. If you want to join them there, you must join them in their faith. And to join them in faith, you must renounce your fig leaves, that is, your own works, and trust wholly in Christ and in His redeeming death.

-11-

From God's Word, the Bible...

Therefore the LORD brought upon them the captains of the army of the king of Assyria, who took Manasseh with hooks, bound him with bronze fetters, and carried him off to Babylon. Now when he was in affliction, he implored the LORD his God, and humbled himself greatly before the God of his fathers, and prayed to Him; and He received his entreaty, heard his supplication, and brought him back to Jerusalem into his kingdom. Then Manasseh knew that the LORD was God.

2 Chronicles 33:11-13

(See also 2 Kings 21:1-18 and 2 Chronicles 33:1-17.)

The Most Surprising Members of the Family (1)

The family of faith includes many, many people that we would have never expected to be part of it. What I'm saying if this: there have been people who were so wicked and ungodly that it would seem to be impossible for them to be saved. If someone had asked us if certain vile, reprehensible people would ever be saved, our answer might very well be: "No, that person is too evil to ever be saved."

I'm talking about people like John Newton. He was such a thoroughly disgusting reprobate that hardly anyone who knew him held out any hope for him. But he was saved by the grace of God, and he is best known to us as the author of the hymn *Amazing Grace*.

It's not enough to put King Manasseh of Judah in the Newton category. He was worse than Newton would ever be. We might say he "out-newtoned" Newton.

Manasseh was a piece of human filth. The son of the godly Hezekiah, Manasseh excelled in evil (2 Kings 21:2,6; 2 Chron. 33:2,9). He was so evil that he even sacrificed his own sons to his false gods (2 Chron. 33:6). Our vocabulary doesn't provide us with enough words to describe this horrible man.

But Manasseh was indeed converted. He came to his senses and turned to God.

How did this surprising change come about? God had spoken to Manasseh on many occasions through various prophets, but Manasseh and the people of Judah "would not listen" (v. 10). When Manasseh ignored the prophets, God did something that he couldn't ignore. He, God, caused Manasseh to be carted off to faraway Babylon with "hooks" and "bronze fetters" (v. 12).

There in Babylon, Manasseh realized what a fool he had been, and he turned to the Lord. He "implored the LORD his God and humbled himself greatly before the God of his fathers" (v. 12).

If there is anything more amazing than Manasseh seeking God, it is God allowing Himself to be found by Manasseh. But that's exactly what God did. He "received his entreaty, heard his supplication, and brought him back to Jerusalem into his kingdom" (v. 13).

I don't doubt for a moment the genuineness of Manasseh's conversion because of these words: "Then Manasseh knew that the LORD was God" (v.13).

How great is the grace of God! We can't calibrate it! God didn't have to put up with Manasseh at all. He could have terminated him as soon as he began to go after idols, but God let him live. God didn't have to send warnings to Manasseh through the prophets, but He did. God didn't have to send affliction upon Manasseh. He could have just let him go on in his sins. And when Manasseh sought Him, the Lord could have turned a deaf ear to his pleas. But God's grace persisted and won the victory over Manasseh!

It's crucial for us to note that Manasseh's conversion manifested itself in a remarkable change of behavior. Manasseh didn't go on living as he had before (vv. 14-16). Many these days seem to think that it is possible for sinners to come to know the Lord and not give any evidence of it. They ignore these words from the Apostle Paul: "Therefore, if anyone is in Christ, he is a new creation; old things have passed away; behold, all things have become new" (2 Cor. 5:17).

The conversion of Manasseh presents us with the following lessons:

- No one is too bad to be saved.
- The way of salvation is to humble ourselves before God, repent of our sins, and ask Him for forgiveness.
- Those who are truly saved will give evidence of it through changed behavior.

When the saved of all the ages gather around the Lord Jesus Christ—wonder of wonders—both Manasseh and John Newton will be there! They may not agree on which of them was the greatest sinner, but they will certainly agree in singing:

> *Amazing grace! how sweet the sound,*
> *That saved a wretch like me!*
> *I once was lost, but now am found,*
> *Was blind, but now I see.*

-12-

From God's Word, the Bible...

And I thank Christ Jesus our Lord who has enabled me, because He counted me faithful, putting me into the ministry, although I was formerly a blasphemer, a persecutor, and an insolent man; but I obtained mercy because I did it ignorantly in unbelief. And the grace of our Lord was exceedingly abundant, with faith and love which are in Christ Jesus. This is a faithful saying and worthy of all acceptance, that Christ Jesus came into the world to save sinners, of whom I am chief. However, for this reason I obtained mercy, that in me first Jesus Christ might show all longsuffering, as a pattern to those who are going to believe on Him for everlasting life. Now to the King eternal, immortal, invisible, to God who alone is wise, be honor and glory forever and ever. Amen.

1 Timothy 1:12-17

The Most Surprising Members of the Family (2)

If we could propel ourselves back in time and land in Acts chapter 8, we would never guess that Saul of Tarsus would become a Christian. There he stands holding the coats of those who are stoning the saintly Stephen. And if we could join him in verses 1 and 2 of Acts chapter 9, our estimate of him would be the same. He is, in the graphic language of verse 1, "still breathing threats and murder against the disciples of the Lord."

If, in our time travel, we could walk the length and breadth of Jerusalem to conduct an opinion poll to discover the least likely man to become a Christian, Saul would win hands down.

Saul hated Christianity with the most utmost hatred. He regarded it as the enemy of the things he most cherished.

As a Pharisee, Saul was looking for the Messiah, but in

his estimation, Jesus wasn't the expected one. As a Pharisee, Saul believed in the resurrection of the dead (in distinction from the Sadducees), but he didn't believe that Jesus arose. He probably held the notion that the disciples of Jesus had made off with His body and fabricated the whole business of a resurrection.

While Saul may not have been completely sure about what happened to Jesus' body, he was completely sure that Christianity had to be stopped in its tracks. He was also sure that he was the very one to do the stopping. Stopper Saul! In fact, he regarded his opposition to Christianity as being the highest service he could render to God.

It all changed when Saul set out for Damascus with visions dancing in his mind of Christians in chains. Saul, the anti-Christian, became a Christian! The Lord Jesus Christ stopped the stopper! A laser beam from heaven flashed around him, blinding him and knocking him to the ground. As he lay groveling in the dust, he heard these words: "Saul, Saul, why are you persecuting Me?" (9:2-3).

Saul immediately knew that he was dealing with the Lord or rather that the Lord was dealing with him. Much to his amazement, he learned that in persecuting Christians, he was actually persecuting the Lord Himself (v. 5). And he also learned that in his mad pursuit of Christians, he was only succeeding in harming himself. He was kicking against "the goads" (v. 5). Goads were sharpened sticks that farmers would attach to the front of their carts. When a stubborn ox rebelled against pulling the cart by kicking it, he soon discovered that there was more pain in kicking than in pulling!

Saul had assessed himself as a terribly enlightened man. Now he learned the Lord's assessment of him—he was a stubborn ox!

It didn't take Saul long to realize that it was time for him to stop kicking and start kneeling in submission to Jesus, and that it was time for him to stop persecuting the people of Jesus and start praying to the Jesus of those people. And pray he did (v. 11).

Saul was soundly converted there on the road to Damascus. He could no longer deny the resurrection of Jesus when the risen Jesus was speaking directly and powerfully to Him! Saul might say to the intellectual skeptics of our day: "You can ridicule the resurrection of Jesus all you want, but when you actually meet Him, your ridicule will end."

Saul of Tarsus, as we know, went on to become the Apostle Paul. From persecutor to preacher! What a change!

Are we surprised that one so opposed to Christ could be saved? We are not as surprised as Paul. He says: "Christ Jesus came into the world to save sinners, of whom I am chief" (1 Tim. 1:15).

If we wear nameplates in heaven (which I seriously doubt), I believe that Paul might ask that his not read "Chief of the Apostles" but rather "Chief of Sinners."

How could the Chief of Sinners get into the family of God? Here is Paul's own answer: "And the grace of our Lord was exceedingly abundant..." (1 Tim. 1:14).

It was grace that showed Paul his sin and pointed him to the Savior. And if in heaven Paul hears Manasseh and John Newton singing *Amazing Grace*, he will certainly say: "Let me help you with that."

.

-13-

From God's Word, the Bible...

And the sons of the prophets said to Elisha, "See now, the place where we dwell with you is too small for us. Please, let us go to the Jordan, and let every man take a beam from there, and let us make there a place where we may dwell." So he answered, "Go."

Then one said, "Please consent to go with your servants." And he answered, "I will go." So he went with them. And when they came to the Jordan, they cut down trees. But as one was cutting down a tree, the iron ax head fell into the water; and he cried out and said, "Alas, master! For it was borrowed."

So the man of God said, "Where did it fall?" And he showed him the place. So he cut off a stick, and threw it in there; and he made the iron float. Therefore he said, "Pick it up for yourself." So he reached out his hand and took it.

2 Kings 6:1-7

The Ax and the Cross

Three things always come to mind when I read the account of the prophet whose ax head went flying into the Jordan River.

First, this was *a seemingly hopeless situation*.

What could be more hopeless than an ax head lying at the bottom of a river? It could not be seen and there was no sonar in those days!

The prophet who lost the ax head certainly realized the gravity of the situation as he cried out to Elisha: "Alas, master! For it was borrowed!" (v. 5).

There was a ton of woe in that one word "Alas"! How could this poor man ever hope to scrape up enough money to pay for the valuable ax head? When he saw it sink, he might very well have exclaimed: "I'm sunk!"

The second major element in this story is *the seemingly senseless solution*.

In turning to Elisha, the forlorn prophet must have been nurturing the hope that he, Elisha, could retrieve what appeared to be irretrievable. He and the other "sons of the prophets" (v. 1) knew that miracles followed Elisha wherever he went. Was a miracle to be had in this situation?

Elisha responded to the young man's cry by merely asking him to point out where the ax head had sunk. Then he "cut off a stick, and threw it in there" (v. 6).

This makes me think of the teacher who said to her students on their first day of school: "If you have to go to the bathroom, raise your hand." One of the students responded: "What good will that do?"

But I'm sure none of the prophets with Elisha made that kind of response. They knew Elisha too well. There were no skeptics there, though there are plenty today. And if Mr. Modern-Day Skeptic had been there, he would have said: "What a stupid thing to do! Throwing a stick into the water! Doesn't it make much more sense to have someone dive into the water and feel around for the ax head?"

Elisha's stick seemed to be completely out of keeping with the seriousness of the problem. The stick was floating on the top, and the ax head was lying at the bottom! What correspondence was there between the two?

But, of course, Mr. Skeptic always leaves God out of the equation, and it was God on whom Elisha was pinning his hope for retrieving the ax head.

The third part of the story is the best part. It is the seemingly hopeless and senseless giving way to salvation—*a surprisingly glorious salvation*.

Elisha's stick went into the water, and the ax head rose to the surface. All the person who had lost it had to do was stoop down and pick it up (v. 7). The ax head was saved from the depths, and the prophet was saved from debt.

Why do we have this account in the Bible? One answer has to do with the original readers of the book. They were captives in Babylon, and there seemed to be no hope that they would ever be released. They were so weak, and Babylon was so strong. It made as much sense to talk about iron floating as it did to talk about release for them. But God saw to it that they were released.

However, we have this account for yet another reason. It was intended by the Holy Spirit to picture salvation for sinners. The Bible tells us that we are all by nature sunk and lost in sin. If it were left to us, our situation would be hopeless. There's no way for us to lift ourselves from the mire of sin. The Bible also gives us the solution for our sin problem, but it seems like such a ridiculous solution. It is none other than Jesus Christ hanging on a cross outside Jerusalem.

Mr. Skeptic looks at that cross and howls in laughter. That cross is the way for sinners to be forgiven of their sins? There seems to be absolutely no connection between Jesus dying there and us lying at the bottom of the river of sin. But that seemingly senseless solution is God's way of salvation. On the basis of that cross, God lifts us from our sin and gives us spiritual life (1 Cor. 1:18-25).

Have you come to the Father in His appointed way of saving sinners—turning away from sin and trusting in Jesus, His Son, and in the work He did on the cross? Jesus spoke these wonderful words recorded in John 6:37: "All that the Father gives Me will come to Me, and the one who comes to Me I will by no means cast out."

-14-

From God's Word, the Bible...

But I fear, lest somehow, as the serpent deceived Eve by his craftiness, so your minds may be corrupted from the simplicity that is in Christ. For if he who comes preaches another Jesus whom we have not preached, or if you receive a different spirit which you have not received, or a different gospel which you have not accepted—you may well put up with it!

2 Corinthians 11:3-4

The Fear of a Churchman

Lots of words come to mind when I think of the Apostle Paul, but fear is not one of them. Quite the opposite! I always associate Paul with boldness.

But in this verse Paul tells us about one of his fears. I call it the fear of a churchman. Churchman? Yes. Paul was a churchman. He loved the church of Jesus Christ with an intense and passionate love, so much so that he placed the good of the church above his personal comfort. He was willing to "spend and be spent" for the church (2 Cor. 12:15). What a testimony! How we need churchmen today! How few there are!

What did Paul, the churchman, fear about the Corinthians? We can divide it into three parts. First, we can say it was *a fear that pertained to the gospel of Christ*. Paul feared that his readers would be "corrupted from the simplicity that is in Christ."

What is the simplicity that is in Christ? I suggest this is

Paul's way of referring to the pure, unadulterated gospel of Christ.

The gospel is the good news of what God has done in and through His Son, Jesus Christ, to rescue sinners from their sins and to give them right standing with Himself now and eternal glory in the future.

What God has done in Christ! Without divesting Himself of His deity (which would be impossible), Jesus took on our humanity. In that humanity, He lived a perfect and sinless life. Then He went to the cross to receive the wrath of God in the place of sinners. He died, but He didn't stay dead. He sprang from the grave in glorious resurrection life. He lives today to make intercession for all who come to God by Him (Heb. 7:25).

What a treasure the gospel is! But the gospel can be adulterated. That brings us to a second aspect of Paul's fear: *It pertained to Satan.*

Paul makes mention of "the serpent" deceiving Eve "by his craftiness." Paul is referring to Genesis 3. There we have the account of Satan coming to Eve in the form of a serpent. He craftily led her into sin.

Satan is still alive and well today, and he has lost none of his craftiness. He hates the gospel with the utmost hatred, and his great goal is to take people away from the truth of it. Paul says he is able to transform himself into "an angel of light," and he has ministers who "transform themselves into ministers of righteousness" (2 Cor. 11:14-15).

The "ministers" Satan was using against the Corinthians were Judaizers. They taught that it was not enough to believe in Jesus in order to be saved. They said it was also necessary to obey the law of Moses. So they were proclaiming a "Christ plus" message. When anyone tells us that we need something in addition to Christ, we can be sure that person is offering a false gospel. It makes me think of these words from my friend Adrian Rogers: "Jesus plus anything is nothing; Jesus plus nothing is everything."

Paul says this message offered "another Jesus," that is, a Jesus plus something else instead of a Jesus plus nothing else. It also created "a different spirit." If we're saved by works, we have reason to be proud and boastful; but if we totally depend on Jesus, we are humbled. And this message amounted to "a different gospel." The word "gospel" means "good news," but there isn't any good news in salvation by works. It is bad news. How can a person ever be sure he or she has done enough to earn salvation? An adulterated gospel was no small thing!

Finally, *Paul's fear pertained to the gullibility of the saints*. Paul was concerned that the Corinthians might "very well put up with" the false gospel of the Judaizers.

Sadly enough, gullible people aren't extinct. They live on. Let a preacher cultivate a highly entertaining style with lots of smiles, jokes, and funny stores, and many listeners will fall for anything he says. Humor in our time is regarded as self-authenticating, that is, if something is funny, that automatically makes it good and right.

In these casual and careless days, we would do well to love the church as Paul loved her, and to fear those things that will harm her. And nothing harms the church more than an adulterated gospel.

-15-

From God's Word, the Bible...

And again He entered Capernaum after some days, and it was heard that He was in the house. Immediately many gathered together, so that there was no longer room to receive them, not even near the door. And He preached the word to them. Then they came to Him, bringing a paralytic who was carried by four men. And when they could not come near Him because of the crowd, they uncovered the roof where He was. So when they had broken through, they let down the bed on which the paralytic was lying.

Mark 2: 1-4

(Please read the whole passage in Mark 2:1-12.)

The Extraordinary

This is an account of the extraordinary. I offer this summary of what we have here—Jesus did extraordinary things when ordinary men took extraordinary measures to meet an extraordinary need. You can easily see that there are four elements in that summary.

Let's begin at the end—*the extraordinary need*. There can be no doubt about that, can there? The man who is brought to Jesus is in a very pathetic condition. Paralyzed! We don't know how long he had been in that condition, but we do know that it would be horrible to be paralyzed for a single hour.

Let's go now to *the extraordinary measures*. We are in the village of Capernaum, and there is much excitement. Jesus is there! Four men are on their way to hear Him, and they come upon this poor paralyzed man. They are immediately touched by his sorrowful condition, and an idea pops into their minds. They will take him to Jesus! This Jesus has healed many (Mark 1:21-45). Perhaps He will heal the paralytic. So they pick up the bed on which the man is lying and head to Jesus. But there's a problem. Jesus is in a packed house.

How can these four men get through the crowd? A solution comes to mind. They will carry him up to the roof—the roof probably consisted of sticks, grass, and dried mud—tear through it, and lower the man to Jesus. I call that taking extraordinary measures.

But the best part of the story is *Jesus doing extraordinary things*. First Jesus assures the man that his sins are forgiven (v. 5). Here's a man who can't even lift his finger to scratch his nose. He needs to be healed, and Jesus is talking about sins being forgiven! Jesus, who always knows better than we, puts first the thing that ought to have priority. He puts the spiritual above the physical. In doing so, Jesus shows us that this man would have been better off to remain paralyzed with his sins forgiven than to be healed of his paralysis and not have his sins forgiven.

After assuring the man of forgiveness, Jesus tells him to get up and pick up. He is to get up from his bed and pick it up. The man obeys, and to his astonished wonder, he is completely healed. And his physical healing was proof that Jesus had the power and authority to heal spiritually (vv. 9-10).

That brings us to the final element in this story—*the ordinary men*, the four men who carry the paralyzed man to Jesus. Who are they? Mark doesn't say. They walk on the stage of Scripture, perform their deed with compassion, resolve, and ingenuity, and then walk off the stage. So far as we know we never meet them again in Scripture. The Holy Spirit, who inspired Mark to write, obviously wanted these men to remain in obscurity. They were probably just ordinary men.

The four elements of the story apply to us. Is there an extraordinary need in this account? There surely is. Do we live in a time of extraordinary need? We surely do. Evil is abounding on every hand, and it's becoming more aggressive and militant. Meanwhile, the Lord's work seems to be languishing.

Our great need is for our Lord to step in and do extraordinary things. How we need a mighty intervention from Him! How we need for Him to step in with saving power for the unconverted and with reviving power for the converted! How we need for Him to vindicate His people and silence the critics!

We know that the mighty moving of God is locked up in His own sovereign purposes and plans. We can't make it occur. But we also know that God's mighty acts usually come when ordinary people, like ourselves, begin to take extraordinary measures. Pastors and churches are certainly taking extraordinary measures these days, most of which come under the heading of entertainment.

The primary measure that we need to take to an extraordinary level is the one ordained by God—prayer! Let us pray much. Let us pray with others. And let us specifically pray for the Lord to do extraordinary things.

-16-

From God's Word, the Bible...

For there is born to you this day in the city of David a Savior, who is Christ the Lord.
Luke 2:11

And the Word became flesh and dwelt among us, and we beheld His glory, the glory as of the only begotten of the Father, full of grace and truth.
John 1:14

Thanks be to God for His indescribable gift!
2 Corinthians 9:15

The Best Christmas Ever

One statement seems to crop up repeatedly each Christmas season—"This is going to be the best Christmas ever." Another form or variation of it goes like this: "This Christmas is going to be perfect."

Every Christmas has to be better than the last one. We are always on the quest for a better Christmas. Everything must be perfect! Nothing must be out of place! Nothing must be allowed to cast a shadow over our celebration!

I want to ask those who toss "the best Christmas ever" around to explain what it is that they're after. What is it that would make this Christmas better than all those that have preceded it? Do we mean that this Christmas we will get the best of all gifts? Do we mean that this Christmas we will see the best of all decorations? Do we mean that we will pull off our contacts with family members and friends without a hitch? Do we mean that we will laugh more? Do we mean that we will eat more? Do we mean that we will go to more Christmas parties?

I'm certainly not opposed to people having an enjoyable Christmas, but I'm not quite sure how to process this endless quest for the best Christmas ever. I wonder if our craving for the "best ever" is really a manifestation of the discontent that has plagued us since Adam and Eve were driven out of Eden. We had the perfect once, but we lost it. And we've been trying to get it back ever since. In other words, I wonder if our yearning for the best Christmas ever really amounts to us saying about ourselves what the Bible says about us.

When I hear "the best Christmas ever" mantra, I want to say: "Give it up! You're too late—two thousand plus years too late!"

The best Christmas ever has already occurred, and it was such a great Christmas that it can never be surpassed. I'm referring, of course, to the very first Christmas, that Christmas without which there would have been no other Christmases.

The first Christmas was the best Christmas because the best of all persons came to this earth to do the best of all things so that we can enjoy the best of all ends.

The best of all persons? That would be the Lord Jesus Christ. Out of all the billions who have occupied Planet Earth, there is no one like Him. He alone qualifies for the title "God-man." God in human flesh! And He came to this earth, not as a full-grown man, but rather as a baby. Who would have thought that God could be held in such a tiny package?

And *the best of all things?* That would be the work of providing salvation for sinners. That work required Him to live in complete obedience to God (by which He provided the righteousness sinners lack), and dying on the cross (in which He received the wrath of God that sinners deserve).

All who believe in Christ rejoice in Him providing the righteousness we don't have and paying for the sins we do have.

What is the best of all ends? It is getting back into the paradise we lost! The theme of the Bible is this: paradise lost through sin and regained through Christ. It is the account of our access to the tree of life being denied because of our sin (Gen. 3:24) and that access being restored through the redeeming work of Christ (Rev. 22:2).

Each Christmas season, we also hear people telling us what Christmas is "all about." Some say it's giving, others say it's family, and yet others say it's having fun. But this is what Christmas is all about: "For God so loved the world that He gave His only begotten Son, that whoever believes in Him should not perish but have everlasting life" (John 3:16).

Is there anything wrong with people desiring to have a better Christmas? No, but the way to make this Christmas better is to think less about it and more about the first Christmas, which was "the best Christmas ever."

-17-

From God's Word, the Bible...

...in everything give thanks; for this is the will of God in Christ Jesus for you.

1 Thessalonians 5:18

When Matthew Henry Was Robbed

Matthew Henry is one of the best-known names in Christian history. Mention his name, and the word "commentary" will come to the minds of almost all pastors and of many church members.

Yes, Matthew Henry wrote a commentary on the entire Bible. It may very well be the most popular of all commentaries. Although Henry died on June 22, 1714, his commentary is still being purchased and used today. I have used it with much profit for many years and still use it.

But it's not his commentary that interests me today. It's rather the day that he was robbed. Can you imagine being confronted by a thief? You're walking along and suddenly someone emerges from the shadows, sticks a knife or a gun in your face, and demands your money. It would be a traumatic event.

Matthew Henry seems to have handled his experience with equilibrium. When asked about it, he said he was glad.

The inquirer must have been floored. Henry had been robbed, and he was glad? He had to ask why. In response Henry gave four reasons for his gladness. The first was that he had never been robbed before. The second was that although the robber took all the money he had, he didn't get much. The third was that the robber had only taken his money and not his life. And the last was that he, Matthew Henry, was the robbed and not the robber.

Matthew Henry had learned to do what the Apostle Paul teaches, that is, to give thanks "in everything."

No, Paul doesn't tell us to give thanks *for* everything. That would require us to endorse all kinds of evil things — war, hatred, hunger, political corruption, disease, sex trafficking, and so on.

It's rather that we are to give thanks *in* everything. The point is this: No matter what comes their way, Christians can always find reasons to be thankful.

We might say Christians are "yes, but" people. "Yes people?" Yes. That means that Christians don't deny the hardships that come their way. They acknowledge them. They don't pretend as if the hardships do not exist or as if they don't hurt. In "pre-political correctness" times, parents would often spank their children. One girl responded to her father spanking her by saying: "That didn't hurt." That wasn't the right thing to say! It prompted the father to say: "Let's try again."

Christians don't deny the hurt of the hardship. When cancer comes to them or a family member, they don't say: "This doesn't hurt." When a friendship fails, they don't say: "This doesn't hurt." When they see society deteriorating through its ungodliness, they don't say: "This doesn't hurt." When they see one of their children rebelling against the Lord, they don't say: "This doesn't hurt."

Yes, Christians are "yes people," but they are also "but

people." Like Matthew Henry, they find reasons to rejoice in the hurt. The truth is that Christians, no matter how severe their hardships are, always have reasons to rejoice, and those reasons are real and substantial.

- Christians can always rejoice in the saving work of the Lord Jesus Christ. The trials of life can never take their salvation away from them (Rom. 8:35-39).
- Christians can always rejoice in the fact that the Lord has promised to be with them in the midst of their difficulties (Heb. 13:5-6). He is there to comfort, strengthen, and sustain.
- Christians can always rejoice in knowing that the Lord who has loved them and saved them has a purpose in allowing trials to come their way, and that purpose is always for their good and His glory (Rom. 8:28). The fact that they can't see God's purpose in the midst of their suffering doesn't mean that it isn't there. Christians trust even when they don't understand, and they look forward to the time when all things will be made clear (1 Cor. 13:12).
- Christians can always rejoice in knowing that a blessed day is coming in which the Lord will remove them from this realm of tears into their eternal home, where there will be no pain, no sorrow, no crying and, thank the Lord, no death! (Rev. 21:1-4).

-18-

From God's Word, the Bible...

John answered and said, "A man can receive nothing unless it has been given to him from heaven. You yourselves bear me witness, that I said, 'I am not the Christ,' but, 'I have been sent before Him.' He who has the bride is the bridegroom; but the friend of the bridegroom, who stands and hears him, rejoices greatly because of the bridegroom's voice. Therefore this joy of mine is fulfilled. He must increase, but I must decrease."

John 3:27-30

(Read the whole passage in John 3:22-36.)

Christ Above All Else

We Christians know that the Lord Jesus Christ is to come first in our lives. The Lord Himself tells us so: "You shall love the Lord your God with all your heart, with all your soul, with all your mind, and with all your strength" (Mark 12:30).

Other Scriptures teach the same (Matt. 6:33; Col. 1:18; 3:1).

Knowing this is one thing. Practicing it is another. There's always something creeping in to keep us from giving the Lord priority. It might be pleasure, possessions or position. It might even be our own family! Yes, we turn our families into idols when we give them the time and the allegiance that belong to the Lord (Matt. 10:37).

Because of the ever-present pressure to shift our priority from the Lord to something else, we need to be reminded of why the Lord should have that priority. In other words, why should we always put the Lord Jesus above all else?

First, the Lord deserves to be put above all else because He came from above.

This was the affirmation of John the Baptist when his disciples expressed unhappiness about Jesus attracting larger crowds (v. 26). John didn't share their view. He knew that he and Jesus were in different categories. John the Baptist was a mere man, but Jesus was the Lord from heaven, and "He who comes from above is above all" (v. 31).

But how do we know for sure that the Lord Jesus came from above? Those who are so eager to disbelieve would do well to consider the birth, the public ministry, the death, and the resurrection of Jesus. His birth indicated His divine nature, being announced by angels (Matt. 1:18-25; Luke 1:26-38; 2:8-14). His public ministry featured many miracles and many kinds of miracles, which were witnessed by many people (John 11:47). His death set off unusual events (Matt. 27:51-54). The closing chapters of each of the four Gospels tell us that Jesus' resurrection was substantiated by many unusual events and many witnesses.

Secondly, the Lord deserves to be put above all else because He has put us above all else.

Why did Jesus come to this earth? It was for the purpose of providing salvation for sinners (Luke 19:10). He didn't have to come, and it was very costly for Him to do so. It required Him to leave the glories of heaven and to endure incredible suffering and anguish in life and in death. But saving us was so important to Him that He put us above His own comfort (2 Cor. 8:9; Phil. 2:5-8).

Thirdly, the Lord Jesus deserves to be put above all else because He has gone above.

Forty days after Jesus arose from the grave, He ascended to the Father in heaven, but it is a mistake to think that He is in heaven today in exactly the same way as He was before He came to this earth. In other words, we must not take a "zip-on, zip-off" view of Jesus' humanity. He didn't "zip on" our humanity for the thirty-three years that He was on this earth so He could take it off at the end of His time here. How many of us miss this point—when Jesus took our humanity, He took it forever. And He is in heaven today in that resurrected body that came out of the grave. The author of Hebrews tells us that Jesus is in heaven as our "forerunner" (Heb. 6:20). The fact that He is in heaven today in resurrected, glorified humanity is the guarantee that all who belong to Him will eventually follow Him into heaven in that same resurrected, glorified humanity (Phil. 3:20-21).

That brings us to the final reason that the Lord Jesus deserves to be put above all else—*He will finally take His people above.*

This world has not seen the last of the Lord Jesus. He will come again, and when He comes He will raise the bodies of dead believers and reunite those bodies to their souls, and He will catch up living believers to meet Him in the air (1 Thess. 4:13-18).

On that day, we shall realize as we never have before how worthy Jesus is to be put above all else, and we will be ashamed of our every failure to do so.

-19-

From God's Word, the Bible...

Be sober, be vigilant; because your adversary the devil walks about like a roaring lion, seeking whom he may devour. Resist him, steadfast in the faith, knowing that the same sufferings are experienced by your brotherhood in the world.

1 Peter 5:8-9

Skunks and Honey Buns

It was eleven o'clock, and my wife was preparing our lunch. She looked out at the backyard and caught a glimpse of something. She couldn't be sure, but she was afraid that she had seen a skunk. All uncertainty was removed a couple of days later. As I was raising the shade on our back door, I saw a skunk ambling along.

Even though our backyard is fenced, we had skunks strolling around. We knew we had to do something. If our dog were to encounter a skunk, it would be disastrous. The stench would be almost impossible to eliminate. And if a skunk were to send his spray directly into our dog's face, she could be permanently blinded.

We had a malodorous problem that had to be dealt with—and dealt with quickly.

So we called an animal control specialist. We had read that skunks can be driven away by putting mothballs out, but the specialist nixed that idea. He told us that setting traps is the only way to deal with this problem. So he pulled a couple of traps out of his truck as I envisioned money flying out of my wallet. The traps worked. In a week's time, we caught, not one, not two, but three skunks.

The interesting thing to me in this process was the bait the specialist used to lure the skunks into the traps—honey buns! If you want to catch skunks, use honey buns. Skunks can't resist them. So said our specialist.

So their craving for those sugary treats was the end for those skunks. Done in by a honey bun—what a way to go!

Our skunk episode set me to thinking about traps and bait. Although I didn't really want to be, I was the enemy of those skunks, and the means I used to kill them was honey buns.

The Bible tells us that we all have an enemy. He is not a reluctant enemy as I was with the skunks. He is a very willing and eager enemy. We know him as Satan or the devil. He was originally one of God's angels, Lucifer by name, and perhaps the greatest of the angels. But he rebelled against God and was cast out of heaven. Now he busies himself with opposing God at every turn. He focuses his attention both on non-Christians and Christians, seeking to keep the former from coming to Christ and the latter from living for Christ.

His stock in trade is subtlety. He doesn't come to us in a blatant way, saying: "I'm the devil, and I'm going to destroy you." If Satan were to come to us in that way, we would flee. The Apostle Paul tells us that Satan uses "wiles"—devious and cunning schemes. We might say that he comes to us with honey buns.

Oftentimes, the honey bun consists of him coming to us in the form of a warm, smiling, affable, and entertaining preacher (2 Cor. 11:13-15) who never tells us that we are sinners who are headed for judgment, and our only hope for salvation lies in the Lord Jesus Christ (John 14:6; Acts 4:12). We snack on the honey bun without realizing that we're being trapped.

Sometimes, the honey bun consists of "the best and the most." In other words, he points us to the elite people of society (the best known and the best educated, and the best situated in material things) and tells us that they believe and live in such and such a way. Then he points us to the most—that is, he tells us that the majority of people believe and live in certain ways. His point is clear: if we don't want to be out of step, we must believe and live as the best and the most.

One of Satan's favorite honey buns is misrepresenting the attributes of God. He, Satan, so elevates God's love that we begin to think God isn't holy or just, that He doesn't care how we live and there are no ill results for not obeying Him.

Satan has many, many more strategies. The thing for us to remember is this: because Satan doesn't lack honey buns, we must not be lacking in discernment.

One of the things that Jesus came to do was to destroy the works of the devil (1 John 3:8). If you are a believer—if you have turned away from sin and are trusting in Christ alone—you may be assured that He will ultimately keep you from the devil's power and deliver you from all evil, but you must be sure to be vigilant!

-20-

From God's Word, the Bible...

But as it is written:
"Eye has not seen, nor ear heard,
Nor have entered into the heart of man
The things which God has prepared for those who love Him."

1 Corinthians 2:9

A Wasted Sheet of Paper

"That man has wasted a sheet of paper!" That was the assessment of Charles M. Alexander, a well-known music director in evangelistic crusades, when he saw Charles H. Gabriel's hymn, *O That Will Be Glory*.

If that was a wasted sheet of paper, I say we need more Gabriels wasting more sheets. There's much to like about this hymn. Here are the first two verses and the chorus:

> *When all my labors and trials are o'er,*
> *And I'm safe on that beautiful shore,*
> *Just to be near the dear Lord I adore*
> *Will through the ages be glory for me.*
>
> *When by the gift of His infinite grace*
> *I am accorded in heaven a place,*
> *Just to be there and to look on His face*
> *Will through the ages be glory for me.*

O that will be glory for me,
Glory for me, Glory for me!
When by His grace I shall look on His face,
That will be glory, be glory for me.

Gabriel didn't look at the world through rose-colored glasses. It's a world of labors and trials. But this world with all of its difficulties and challenges is not permanent. God's people are destined to land "safe on that beautiful shore." Heaven will be far more beautiful than we have ever imagined, but the best part of it will be enjoying nearness to the Lord who brought us there, and, as the second verse says, to "look on His face." The best sight in heaven will be the sight of Christ (Ps. 17:15).

Don't you love that word "safe"? Safe on that beautiful shore! Safe from sin! Safe from Satan! Safe from the world! Safe from doubt! Safe from fear! Safe from sorrow, pain, and death! Safe!

How do we get to heaven? How are we "accorded in heaven a place"? It is all due, Gabriel says, to "the gift of His infinite grace." No one in heaven will take credit for being there. No one will be boasting that he was smarter than those who aren't there. No one will say that he had enough sense to figure it all out while others didn't. Everyone there will boast in God's grace. All will realize that it was grace that caused them to see their sin and to tremble at the thought of standing before a holy God. All will realize that it was God's grace that pointed to the perfect life and the substitutionary death of Christ as the only way for their sins to be forgiven. All will realize that even the faith with which they received that salvation was God's gift (Eph. 2:8-9; Phil. 1:29). No one in heaven will dare say: "God deserves part of the credit, and I deserve part of the credit for salvation." Each will rather say:

> *'Twas grace that taught my heart to fear,*
> *And grace my fears relieved.*
> (John Newton, *Amazing Grace*)

Three times in his hymn Gabriel uses the phrase "through the ages." Heaven will last through endless ages. Newton's hymn puts it in these words:

> *When we've been there ten thousand years,*
> *Bright shining as the sun;*
> *We've no less days to sing God's praise*
> *Than when we first begun.*

Then there's that phrase "glory for me," which Gabriel uses repeatedly. What does he mean? He's not only saying that he will be in the glory (the magnificence and splendor) of heaven, but heaven's glory will be in him. In other words, he will be taking tremendous delight in it. He will relish it and revel in it. He will exult in it, that is, he will feel elation and jubilation. Being in the glory of heaven will cause God's people to glorify Him.

This was Gabriel's testimony. Is it ours? Can we each say "glory for me"? Do we have the assurance that we will be in heaven? To have that assurance we must have the Lord Jesus as our Savior, and the only way we can have Him is to repent of our sins and trust in Him.

Now let's get back to Charles Alexander. He began hearing Gabriel's song wherever he went. So he changed his mind about it, and even used it as the theme song in a crusade he did with R.A. Torrey. It turns out that Gabriel didn't waste that sheet of paper after all.

-21-

From God's Word, the Bible...

Therefore we must give the more earnest heed to the things we have heard, lest we drift away. For if the word spoken through angels proved steadfast, and every transgression and disobedience received a just reward, how shall we escape if we neglect so great a salvation, which at the first began to be spoken by the Lord, and was confirmed to us by those who heard Him, God also bearing witness both with signs and wonders, with various miracles, and gifts of the Holy Spirit, according to His own will?

Hebrews 2:1-4

Christians Neglecting Salvation

For years I assumed the question of verse 3 is addressed to unbelievers. I read it like this: "Sinners, how will you escape hell if you neglect the salvation provided by the Lord Jesus?"

It finally occurred to me that the words "sinners" and "hell" are not in the question. I had been reading them into the question.

It is, of course, very important to ask sinners that question, but the author of Hebrews isn't addressing unbelievers in this passage. He's addressing his fellow believers. Notice how he includes himself with them by using the words "we" (vv. 1, 3) and "us" (v. 3).

Salvation is a much greater matter than merely "accepting Christ." It's not just a decision. It's a life. It's an ongoing thing. And the truth is Christians can neglect it. Just as we can neglect our families, so we Christians can and do neglect our relationship with the Lord.

This is how the man who wrote this epistle was assessing his readers, who were Jews who had come to faith in Christ. They were neglecting their walk with the Lord. So he writes to ask them to think about where this will lead them. How shall they "escape" if they continue to do this? Escape what? The answer, I suggest, is in verse two where he mentions "a just reward."

What is the "just reward" for a Christian who neglects his or her Lord? The author doesn't spell it out for us here, but later in the epistle we find him warning his readers about the chastisement or discipline of the Lord (12:3-11).

His message to neglectful Christians is this: "Watch out! By neglecting the Lord, you're inviting Him to chastise you as a father chastises his children."

We don't like to believe that God chastises His people, but this author assures us that He does so. In a quotation from Psalm 94:12, the author says:

> *"For whom the Lord loves He chastens,*
> *And scourges every son whom He receives"*
> (Heb. 12:6)

God's chastisement is never pleasant, but it's always for our good (Heb. 12:11). It plays a much larger role in the Christian life than we realize. What form does chastisement take? It can come in the form of God sending adversity our way or God withholding blessings from us. Or it can be a combination of the two.

But let's get back to this matter of Christians neglecting their salvation. How does this come about? We find the answer in the word "drift" (Heb. 2:1). In this world, there are always plenty of currents to pull us away from the Lord, and if we don't put forth the effort to swim against those currents, away we shall go. We get busy and absorbed with our careers and our pleasures. We allow ourselves to become enamored with the latest trends. We socialize with people who don't share our faith. These and many other things can carry us away from Christ. We must be aware and beware.

I can boil it down to this: we are either putting forth effort in the Christian life or we are drifting. There are no other options. What does it mean to put forth effort in the Christian life? It means reading and studying the Scriptures, being diligent in prayer, and attending worship services in Bible-based, Christ-honoring churches.

What should we do if we have been drifting away from Christ? The author answers that question in these words: "give the more earnest heed" (v. 1). That means "pay more attention." If we are drifting in our walk with the Lord, we need to pay more attention to it. We need to repent and start doing again those things that will draw us close to the Lord.

The best way to avoid drifting is to continually reflect on the greatness of our salvation. The biblical authors could never mention salvation without stressing the wonder and the glory of it. Sadly enough, it's possible to be around lots of Christians these days without getting the impression they possess something that is truly glorious.

If we're drifting from the Lord, we don't need to get our salvation back. It's impossible for us to lose it. But we do need to get the glory of it back.

-22-

From God's Word, the Bible...

On the twenty-fourth day of the eleventh month, which is the month Shebat, in the second year of Darius, the word of the LORD came to Zechariah the son of Berechiah, the son of Iddo the prophet: I saw by night, and behold, a man riding on a red horse, and it stood among the myrtle trees in the hollow; and behind him were horses: red, sorrel, and white. Then I said, "My lord, what are these?" So the angel who talked with me said to me, "I will show you what they are."
And the man who stood among the myrtle trees answered and said, "These are the ones whom the LORD has sent to walk to and fro throughout the earth."

Zechariah 1:7-10

(Read the whole passage in Zechariah 1:7-17.)

The Red Horse in the Myrtle Grove

For many years, I didn't pay much attention to the prophecy of Zechariah. It seemed to be impossible to understand. I finally decided to give it a thorough study. I'm glad I did; that study brought the book alive to me.

My favorite part of the prophecy is Zechariah's vision of the red horse in the myrtle grove. This is the first of eight visions in the book.

Myrtle trees are well known for the darkness of their shade, and in this vision we have a whole grove of these trees. And the grove is situated in a valley. This part of the vision conveys darkness—deep, deep darkness. It was a very fitting emblem for the people to whom Zechariah was ministering. These people had returned to their homeland from captivity in Babylon. They came back with great joy and zeal. They understood why their people had been in captivity. It was because they had forsaken the Lord and gone after idols. They were now determined that they would serve the Lord. They immediately set to work to rebuild the temple. But the pressing demands of their own lives and the hostility of neighboring nations began to take their toll. In addition to those things, the realization hit them that the temple they were building couldn't begin to compare to the original temple built by Solomon.

So they stopped working on the temple for fourteen years. Zechariah was one of the prophets God used to call them away from their apathy and to spur them on to resuming their work.

Those people might have described their situation in this way: It's like living in the dark shade in a dark hollow. That also seems to be an appropriate way to describe the church today. She is despised by the world, and she seems to be making precious little progress in advancing the gospel. It is a time in which we could say the devil's wolves are very wolfish, and the Lord's sheep are very sheepish.

That brings us to the heartwarming, soul-thrilling part of the vision. There was in that hollow a man riding a red horse, and with Him were others riding on horses of various colors (v. 8). We should understand these riders to be the angels of the Lord.

The rider on the red horse is none other than the Lord Himself. He is identified as "the Angel of the LORD" (v. 11), who is simply called God in other passages (Gen. 22:15-16; Exod. 3:2,6; Judg. 6:22; 13:21-22).

Here are blessed consolations. The Lord is with His people in their afflictions and sorrows. And He is not lacking in resources to help His people. Other riders are with Him, and, as the passage makes clear, are ready to receive orders from Him (vv. 10-11).

The fact that the Lord is riding a red horse suggests that He is not ambivalent or neutral about the sad condition of His people. Red, the color of blood, speaks of war. The Lord is among His people to fight on their behalf. We cannot doubt this for one simple reason: the Lord has already gone into the greatest battle of all on behalf of His people! He has gone to the cross to defeat the enemy of their souls, Satan, and to secure for them eternal salvation.

The most consoling part of this passage is found in the fact that the Lord Himself intercedes for his people. Zechariah hears him cry out to God: "O LORD of hosts, how long will You not have mercy on Jerusalem and on the cities of Judah, against which You were angry these seventy years?" (v. 12).

The church's greatest resource in the midst of her difficulties isn't the wisdom of her leaders or the attractiveness of her programs. It's always the intercession of the Christ who laid down His life for her. And the God who sent Christ to die for her can never disregard His Son's intercession on her behalf.

Does the church today seem to be in the dark shade of dark trees in a dark hollow? Let's cry to the Lord to show His zeal and bestow His mercy. Let's join our pleas with Christ's until such a season comes.

-23-

From God's Word, the Bible...

"Let not the wise man glory in his wisdom,
Let not the mighty man glory in his might,
Nor let the rich man glory in his riches;
But let him who glories glory in this,
That he understands and knows Me,
That I am the LORD, exercising lovingkindness, judgment, and righteousness in the earth.
For in these I delight," says the LORD.

Jeremiah 9:23-24

Propitiation and Diapers

I recall a sermon I heard many years ago. The preacher took as his text Paul's wonderful words in Romans 3:21-26 and focused on the word "propitiation."

Propitiation is one of the most glorious words in the New Testament. It takes us to the very core of what the Lord Jesus was doing when He died on the cross.

The word reminds us of our dilemma. Because of our sins, we deserve the wrath of God. Our only hope is for the wrath of God to be propitiated, that is, to be satisfied or appeased so that God is not angry with us any longer.

That's precisely what Jesus did on the cross. He received the wrath of God in the place of sinners, and He received it to the extent that God was propitiated.

I watched the congregation as he preached. Their response was not so much one of boredom as it was of blandness. While the listeners weren't objecting to what he was saying, they certainly weren't awed or overwhelmed by it.

Toward the end of his sermon, the preacher included an illustration that had to do with him and his wife needing to buy diapers for their little one before beginning a trip. It seems that they ran into all kinds of difficulties in trying to do this simple task.

I noticed the shift in the attentiveness of the congregation when he began sharing this illustration. The blandness went away, and the hearers immediately began to sit up, lean forward and smile.

Preachers enjoy getting good responses from their listeners, and illustrations are good for getting favorable responses. But while illustrations are necessary, they can be detrimental. When we preachers see we're getting lots of smiles and laughter from an illustration, we have a tendency to embellish it, and it begins to take on a life of its own. Suddenly, the illustration has ceased to serve the sermon, and now the sermon is serving the illustration. Someone has observed that illustrations are to the sermon what windows are to a house. As windows bring light into the house, so illustrations are to bring light into the sermon—but we don't want a house to be all windows.

The man who preached this sermon is a good and faithful preacher. I don't fault him for using this particular illustration even though I don't remember how he tied it in to the matter of propitiation. The thing that I found disconcerting was how we in the congregation were more interested in the misadventures associated with buying the diapers than we were in the propitiation of Christ. We quite obviously found something of a trivial and mundane nature to be very riveting, and yet the propitiation of Christ, well, not so much.

It should concern us that many pastors have gone exclusively into the business of elevating the trivial and mundane over the glorious. No need to ever expect a sermon on propitiation from such pastors! Christianity is about converting sinners, but they have converted Christianity by turning it into a successful living technique in which we get God to be our personal errand boy. They offer us a God who will take care of whatever life throws our way, conveniently ignoring that many of these things (such as managing our busy, busy schedules) are things we can—and should—do for ourselves.

Meanwhile, the great message of the Bible is God doing for us what we cannot do for ourselves. It is Christ satisfying the wrath of God on the cross on our behalf. The only way we can ever satisfy that wrath is by being eternally separated from Him. Thank God, the propitiatory work of the Lord Jesus means all who entrust themselves to Him in that work never have to worry about that eternal separation. God is propitiated, and they are saved!

Glory in buying diapers if you wish, but let me let me glory in the Lord Jesus Christ.

> *I will glory in my Redeemer*
> *Whose priceless blood has ransomed me*
> *Mine was the sin that drove the bitter nails*
> *And hung Him on that judgment tree*
> *I will glory in my Redeemer*
> *Who crushed the power of sin and death*
> *My only Savior before the Holy Judge*
> *The Lamb Who is my righteousness*
> *The Lamb Who is my righteousness.*[3]

---

[3] I will glory in my Redeemer, Steve and Vikki Cook, http://sovereigngracemusic.org/music/songs/i-will-glory-in-my-redeemer/

-24-

From God's Word, the Bible...

Now the Angel of the LORD came and sat under the terebinth tree which was in Ophrah, which belonged to Joash the Abiezrite, while his son Gideon threshed wheat in the winepress, in order to hide it from the Midianites. And the Angel of the LORD appeared to him, and said to him, "The LORD is with you, you mighty man of valor!"

Gideon said to Him, "O my lord, if the LORD is with us, why then has all this happened to us? And where are all His miracles which our fathers told us about, saying, 'Did not the LORD bring us up from Egypt?' But now the LORD has forsaken us and delivered us into the hands of the Midianites."

Judges 6:11-13

A Man in a Vise (1)

Gideon was a man in a vise. Ah, you're thinking that I don't I know how to spell "vice." Sometimes I don't know how to spell, but in this case my spelling is correct. A "vice'" is wicked or immoral behavior, but a "vise" is a tool with movable jaws. Place an item between those jaws, turn the handle until they firmly grip or clamp the item, and it won't go anywhere.

Now Gideon was not in a vise in a literal sense. No one was clamping him between the iron jaws of a tool. I'm using the vise as a figure or picture of the dilemma in which Gideon found himself.

One "jaw" of Gideon's vise consisted of the Midianites. For seven long years they had made life miserable for the people of Israel. Judges 6:2-6 says it all: "the hand of Midian prevailed against Israel… so Israel was greatly impoverished because of the Midianites."

The other "jaw" was God. Gideon thought that the Lord should have done something about the Midianites, but He hadn't. After all, the Lord had delivered Israel from her enemies on previous occasions and, indeed, had promised to do so (Lev. 26:7-8; Deut. 28:7). So Gideon was upset because the Midianites were doing all kinds of things and the Lord was doing nothing!

Gideon was "squeezed" between the activity of the Midianites and the inactivity of God. He was a man of faith (vv. 11-13), but his faith didn't seem to be accomplishing anything. It didn't seem to be working very well.

Are you able to identify with Gideon? Do you find yourself surrounded and assailed by the cruel "Midianites" of life—and God doesn't seem to care?

What are believers to do when their faith seems not to be working? Gideon can help us. He rises from the pages of Scripture to teach us valuable lessons about faith. This reading deals with the first of these and the next reading with two others

The first lesson we learn from Gideon about faith is this: *We must examine our faith to make sure we are not trying to make God do something He has not obligated Himself to do.*

Do we understand faith? Faith isn't a matter of believing that God will do whatever we want done. It's not "positive thinking." Faith is rather a matter of believing that God will do what He has promised to do in the time and manner that suits Him. In other words, we cannot have faith apart from the Word of God (Romans 10:17).

Gideon was in a crisis of faith because he had been expecting God to do something about the Midianites. Gideon wanted them removed from the scene and he seems to have convinced himself that God was obligated to do this. But it was God who had sent those very Midianites! We read, "Then the children of Israel did evil in the sight of the LORD. So the LORD delivered them into the hand of Midian for seven years" (v. 1).

The people of Israel were in a covenant relationship with

God. One part of that covenant was God's pledge to give Israel victory over her enemies. This is evidently what Gideon had in mind. But there was another part to that same covenant, namely, Israel's responsibility to obey God's commandments. Under the covenant of Sinai, God was not obligated to keep His promise to deliver Israel from her enemies if she did not obey His laws.

In particular, God had made it clear that Israel must not worship and serve other gods. Idolatry would not bring Israel victory over her enemies but bondage to them (Deut. 28:25). So the Midianites who vexed them were proof not of the Lord's failure to deliver but rather that God keeps His word!

Gideon's mistake was to separate God's blessings from Israel's responsibilities. We often do the same. We want God to bless us regardless of the way we live—and when we don't get the blessings we want and expect, we conclude that God has failed.

As always, the Lord Jesus is our example. The blessing put before Him was that of seeing His people redeemed, but that could only be achieved by His death on the cross. So Jesus embraced both the responsibility and the blessing.

-25-

From God's Word, the Bible...

Then the LORD turned to him and said, "Go in this might of yours, and you shall save Israel from the hand of the Midianites. Have I not sent you?"

Judges 6:14

A Man in a Vise (2)

This reading brings us to two additional lessons that Gideon teaches us about faith. The first of these two lessons is this: *It's always too early to give up on God.*

For seven long years the Midianites had oppressed Israel. It is probably safe to say that Gideon and other people of faith spent much of those seven years wondering why God did nothing to change the situation.

But suddenly Gideon finds himself in the presence of the very God that he had been wondering about (vv. 11-12).

The Lord announces that He is now ready to deliver Israel from the Midianites.

Gideon's experience warns us to beware of "snapshot theology." God's work in this world is like a movie. But we oftentimes look at a single clip—a snapshot—and start making pronouncements.

We see the clip and wonder why God has done this or that, and why He hasn't done the other. We're so sure that we're seeing everything and that we're right in our conclusions, but we are looking only at a single snapshot. God tells us to watch the whole movie and He assures us that everything will make perfect sense at the end of it all. These lines express it well:

> *It will be worth it all when we see Jesus.*
> *Life's trials will seem so small when we see Him.*
> *One glimpse of His dear face*
> *All sorrow will erase.*
> *So let us run the race*
> *Till we see Christ.*
> (Esther Kerr Rusthoi)

Here is the final lesson Gideon teaches us about faith: *We must feed our faith on the faithfulness of God.*

The Lord had work for Gideon to do: "Go in this might of yours, and you shall save Israel from the hand of the Midianites. Have I not sent you?" (v. 14).

Gideon was to be God's instrument to achieve God's purpose. He was to be God's man to triumph over the enemy and to secure that victory on behalf of all His people.

The people of Israel were suffering because they had broken the covenant of Sinai. But long before Sinai, the Lord had established a covenant with Abraham—a covenant of promise (Gal. 3:16-18). The centerpiece of that covenant was God's promise to send a Mediator—who would be God's own Son and would come to this earth to save a rebellious people from their sins (Matt. 1:23). He would come to secure victory over Satan on their behalf.

In Israel, the people of faith held to this belief in a coming Savior. Yes, there were times when their faith in that promise would diminish. The seven years of Midianite oppression was such a time. But then God would raise up a man like Gideon to deliver Israel—and people of faith would see in that deliverer a reminder or preview of the great Deliverer who was to come. So their faith would be rekindled and renewed.

How does this help us when we feel that our faith is not working? It gives us something on which to feed our faith so that it will begin to work again! The fact that God kept His promise to send His Son demonstrates His faithfulness.

When we feel that our faith isn't working, we should think about the faithfulness of God, and we should think about it in a particular way. The sending of His Son to be our Savior is God's great promise. Since God was faithful in keeping that great promise, we should never doubt that He will keep all of His lesser promises. Faith always lets the greater thing govern the lesser things.

Does it seem to you that your faith isn't working? Let Gideon help you. Look at his life and be reminded that:

- true faith does not try to obligate God to do what He has not promised;
- true faith doesn't give up on God because of what it sees at the moment; and
- true faith looks to the redeeming work of Christ as proof that God will never fail to keep His promises.

Armed with these truths, our faith can forge ahead in a world that might otherwise make it seem pointless.

-26-

From God's Word, the Bible...

Now Gideon perceived that He was the Angel of the LORD. So Gideon said, "Alas, O Lord GOD! For I have seen the Angel of the LORD face to face."

Judges 6:22

Focusing Faith (1)

The place to thresh wheat was on a threshing floor, a high place where the thresher could let the wind blow the chaff away. Gideon is threshing wheat, but not on a threshing floor. He is nestled down in a winepress. The winepress, a depressed site, enables him to stay low and out of sight. Why is Gideon wanting to keep out of sight? The Midianites are making life miserable for the Israelites.

When the Angel of the LORD speaks to him, Gideon begins complaining about those Midianites. He is whining in the winepress! Gideon is a man of faith, but at this point his faith isn't working very well. He cannot understand why God is not doing something about those Midianites.

We can easily identify with Gideon. Our faith sometimes sputters and stalls. What are we to do when that is the case?

One thing we learn from Gideon is to focus on God and not on the Midianites. When we meet Gideon, he is so focused on the Midianites that all he can see is Midianites. If we were in his situation, we would probably be just like he was.

The big thing that happens in the verses before us is this: God shifts Gideon's focus away from the Midianites and on Himself. He does so by appearing to him as the Angel of the LORD. We should probably understand this to mean that God temporarily took human flesh to appear to Gideon.

Gideon soon realizes that he is in the presence of the very God that he had been complaining about! When Gideon realizes he in God's presence, the issue is no longer the Midianites. It's rather how he, Gideon, could stand before such a God (v. 22). The Midianites suddenly get lost in the glory of God!

We have our own Midianites, don't we? We have our problems, and at times they are so severe that they take over all of life. We can't think about anything else. With "Midianites" swarming all around us, it's hard for us to see anything else. And the more we look at those "Midianites," the more there are and the bigger they seem. Our urgent need in such times is to look to God. We do no harm if we slightly re-work the words of a familiar hymn:

Turn your eyes upon Jesus,
Look full in His wonderful face;
And the "Midianites" of life will grow strangely dim
In the light of His glory and grace.

Think about Simon Peter for a moment. He's looking at the Lord and walking on the water toward Him. But then he begins to look at those waves rolling around him, and he starts to sink (Matt. 14:22-33). It's when we take our eyes off the Lord to look at the "Midianites" that we begin to sink.

The Lord gives Gideon no choice about this matter of focusing on Him and His glory. He accommodates Gideon's request for a sign by causing fire to burst from a rock to consume Gideon's lunch (v. 21). We might find ourselves thinking how much easier it would be for us to shift our attention from our problems to the Lord if He would only do a miracle for us.

The truth of the matter is that the Lord has done so much more for us. We have even greater signs. The Lord who appears only briefly to Gideon comes again as a baby in the tiny village of Bethlehem. He comes to dwell on this earth for several years. He comes to die on the cross for sinners like us. He comes to rise in victory from the grave and to ascend in resurrected humanity to the Father in heaven. The glory of the redeeming work of Christ is greater than the glory of fire leaping from a rock!

When the trials and adversities of life mount up all around us, the very best thing we can do is look at Jesus' redeeming work until we are once again "lost in wonder, love and praise." That look won't make the "Midianites" go away, but it will surely make them shrink in size before our eyes. It will make marauding "Midianites" manageable "Midianites."

-27-

From God's Word, the Bible...

*Now it came to pass the same night that the LORD said to him,
"Take your father's young bull, the second bull of seven years old,
and tear down the altar of Baal that your father has, and cut down
the wooden image that is beside it;
and build an altar to the LORD your God. . ."*

Judges 6:25-26a

Focusing Faith (2)

Gideon teaches us when our faith is in crisis to refocus. We're to shift our focus away from the crisis to the Lord Himself. We can put it like this: when we're facing the fierce "Midianites" of life, we're to focus on the Lord and not on the "Midianites."

But there's yet another truth for us to learn on this matter of refocusing our faith, that is, we are to focus more on the enemy within than on the enemy without.

Prior to the Lord's visit, Gideon is aware of only one enemy—the enemy without. Those Midianites! The Lord's appearance turns his attention to a much more dangerous and sinister enemy—the one within! And what is the enemy within? It is devotion to idols.

After departing from Gideon that day, the Lord returns in the evening with this command: "…tear down the altar of Baal that your father has, and cut down the wooden image that is beside it; and build and altar to the LORD your God…" (vv. 25b-26a).

So now we see Gideon has a problem much closer to

home than the Midianites! He has been saying to God: "Why don't you do something about those Midianites?" And here we have the Lord saying to him: "Why don't you do something about idols?"

The Midianites that Gideon so dreaded and feared were caused by the idolatry of the Israelites. The Lord was sending the Midianites upon Israel as His judgment on their idolatry. The idols were causing the Midianites, and the idols must be removed before the Midianites could be removed. Here the Lord makes it clear to Gideon that he must take the lead in this matter of getting rid of idols.

The major idol of Gideon's day was Baal—a nature god who was supposed to ensure the fertility of the land and, hence, good crops. So he was the god of affluence and comfort. We don't worship Baal by that name today, but we do love our affluence and comfort. So we are still worshiping him after all.

An idol is anything that receives from us what properly belongs to God. When we give to anything else the time that belongs to the Lord, we have an idol. When we give to anything else the money that belongs to the Lord, we have an idol. When we give to anything else the love and affection that belong to the Lord, we have an idol.

How very easy it is for us to go about blaming our "Midianites" while we refuse to address our own idolatry! Let someone ask why our society is in its present lamentable condition, and we eagerly point to the political leaders, the judicial system, and to the entertainment industry. Meanwhile the Lord is telling those of us who belong to Him to look at the idolatry in our midst.

When society is deteriorating and in need of healing, we who are God's people are called not to sign petitions and organize politically, but rather to humble ourselves, pray, seek God's face, and turn from our wicked ways (2 Chron. 7:14).

There's nothing wrong with Christians being politically involved as long as they understand that the answer to society's ill can never be politics without God.

We are so very much like Gideon. We want God to do what we think He should do, but we're not quite as eager to do what we should do. It's always easier for us to blame God than it is to deny our own Baals.

What, then, are we to do when our faith is in crisis, when it seems not to be working? Gideon rises from the pages of Scripture to tell us to focus on God and on our own sins instead of on the "Midianites" that trouble us. Faith always works well when it is lubricated with the glory of God and when its gears are free from the sand of sin. And let us ever look to the Lord Jesus as the example of what it means to live for God's glory and without sin. We can't ever be perfect as He was, but we can always seek to be more like Him.

-28-

From God's Word, the Bible...

Then the LORD said to Gideon, "By the three hundred men who lapped I will save you, and deliver the Midianites into your hand. Let all the other people go, every man to his place."

Judges 7:7

Faith Keeps in Mind the Big Picture

Judges 7 begins with God preparing Gideon to face the Midianites and ends with God giving Gideon victory over them. But there's something here of even greater significance, that is, several insights into those things that cause faith to work as it should. This chapter provides us with pictures of those things that we must keep in mind for our faith to work. We look at the first of these three things in this reading and the remaining two in the next reading.

First, for faith to work it must keep in mind the big picture (vv. 2-8).

The big picture is supplied for us by the Lord commanding Gideon to reduce the number of his soldiers. Gideon has managed to muster an army of 32,000. That number must have seemed to him to be the bare minimum against the 135,000 of the Midianites. But just as he is assuring himself that victory might very well be possible with his 32,000, the Lord shows up to tell him to send all the cowards home.

Gideon may very well have consoled himself with the thought that only a hundred or two would fall into that category, still leaving him an army of over 30,000. But get this: 22,000 gladly placed themselves in the "coward" category, got up, and went home! This shows us how little of faith there was in Israel at the time.

How could any army of 10,000 possibly succeed against the Midianites? We can imagine Gideon furiously scratching out a battle plan on the back of an envelope. Maybe it could still work! But God isn't through. He shows up again to say: "The people are still too many…" (v. 4).

By this time Gideon has learned enough about God to obey, even though questions were screaming within him. If the Lord wanted a further reduction, a further reduction there would be. But how was it to be made? The Lord gave the answer. Gideon was to take his 10,000 down to the water to drink. Those who put their faces into the water were to be sent home. Those who scooped the water and drank from their hands were to stay.

Imagine Gideon's consternation as he watched! Thousands put their faces into the water. When the drinking was done, Gideon had an army of 300! He may have been thinking that he would have been better off with 22,000 cowards!

We must not give these 300 men too much credit. Some think God wanted them because they showed by their drinking that they were more watchful and alert. But, no, the 300 weren't superior to the others. How do we know this? Because God was determined that Israel wouldn't take any credit for the forthcoming victory. All the glory would go to God alone (v. 2). So the method of separation was entirely arbitrary.

We have, then, what I call the big picture. It is the glory of God.

When our faith doesn't seem to be working, it's often because we've lost sight of the glory of God. In other words, we've lost sight of what God is working toward. We want to believe He's working to make our lives comfortable and easy. And when our lives are not comfortable and easy, we think God isn't doing His job, and our faith wavers.

If we begin with the wrong job description for God, He will always fail in our eyes. We have a tendency to think His job description is to secure our comfort, but it's actually to glorify Himself. It's wrong for us to seek our glory, but that's because we're sinful. God is perfect, and as a perfect being He must seek His glory or He would no longer be perfect.

In the pursuit of His glory, God sometimes brings difficult circumstances our way. If we handle them as we should, He is glorified. Strong faith interprets all circumstances in light of the glory of God, and faith is most satisfied when God is most glorified.

By the way, God has determined in the matter of saving sinners exactly the same as He did about delivering Israel from Midian, that is, that no one will be able to say "My own hand has saved me" (v. 2). Salvation is entirely the work of God. As sinners, we can be confident in His perfect work for us in Christ. Through His life on earth and His death at Calvary, the Lord Jesus Christ will bring us safely home to His heavenly kingdom at last.

-29-

From God's Word, the Bible...

And when Gideon had come, there was a man telling a dream to his companion. He said, "I have had a dream:
To my surprise, a loaf of barley bread tumbled into the camp of Midian; it came to a tent and struck it so that it fell and overturned, and the tent collapsed."
Then his companion answered and said, "This is nothing else but the sword of Gideon the son of Joash, a man of Israel! Into his hand God has delivered Midian and the whole camp."

Judges 7:13-14

Faith Keeps in Mind the Hidden Picture and the Final Picture

We're looking at those things faith must keep in mind if it is to avoid being in a crisis, and if it is to work well. Yesterday's reading made the first point that *for faith to work, it must see the big picture*. The second thing is this: *for faith to work well it must keep in mind the hidden picture* (vv. 9-18).

What is the hidden picture? It is that God is always at work in unusual places and in unusual ways. Faith falters when we think that we are seeing the whole picture, and when it seems that God is nowhere to be found in that picture.

When we first encounter Gideon, he is quite discouraged because God didn't appear to be doing much (6:13). And now standing there with what is left of his army, Gideon has reason to believe God still isn't doing very much! But he is about to get a different perspective as God commands him to sneak into the camp of the Midianites on that very night (vv. 9-11).

When Gideon arrives, he is in for quite a surprise. One Midianite is talking about a dream in which he had seen a barley cake tumbling into the camp of Midian, striking a tent and knocking it to the ground (v. 13). The man with whom the Midianite is sharing his dream isn't in doubt about its meaning: "This is nothing else but the sword of Gideon the son of Joash, a man of Israel; for into his hand God delivered Midian and the whole camp" (v. 14).

The barley cake—the common cake eaten by common people—was Gideon. The tent was Midian. The barley cake destroyed the tent. Gideon would defeat the Midianites! The interesting thing is that the very same God who had been working with Gideon was also working on the other side of the fence. While He was encouraging the one (Gideon), He was demoralizing the other (the Midianites). Gideon had been totally unaware of this until his trip into the Midianite camp. It has been hidden from him! What a blessed lesson there is for us in this! God is always doing more than we think, and His doing is always for our good and for His glory (Rom. 8:28).

The third lesson for us to learn about faith working well is this: *For faith to work well it must keep in mind the final picture* (vv. 19-25).

After visiting the camp of Midian, Gideon must have returned to his little army with the utmost confidence. God would indeed give them the victory! And God did exactly that, going about it in a most unusual and unexpected way. Armed with nothing more than trumpets, pitchers, and torches, the army of Israel prevailed. The trumpets were blown, the pitchers were shattered, the torches glowed, and the 300 soldiers cried: "The sword of the LORD and of Gideon!" (v. 20). The Midianites, completely bewildered and disoriented, were put to flight!

God ever delights in using unlikely instruments to achieve enormous things. Outside the city of Jerusalem stands a cross, and on that cross hangs a carpenter who has become a rabbi. The world laughs at that cross, but God used that unlikely instrument to bring eternal salvation to all who believe. God will continue to use that cross to bring salvation, and all those who are saved will finally come into the glory of His presence. Satan will be defeated, and the Lord of glory will triumph. The redeemed will gladly join in singing:

> *Worthy is the Lamb who was slain*
> *To receive power and riches and wisdom,*
> *And strength and honor and glory and blessing!*
> (Rev. 5:14)

I rejoice that the Holy Spirit, the ultimate author of Scripture, saw fit to include the account of Gideon. We certainly need it. Our faith, like his, is often weak and trembling. When my faith is that way, nothing helps me more than thinking about the *big* picture (the glory of God), the *hidden* picture (God is at work even when He doesn't seem to be), and the *final* picture (God will make sure His cause and His people triumph). Faith works well when it looks at things through those three lenses.

-30-

From God's Word, the Bible...

And now my head shall be lifted up above my enemies all around me;
Therefore I will offer sacrifices of joy in His tabernacle;
I will sing, yes, I will sing praises to the LORD.
Psalm 27:6

Make a joyful shout to the LORD, all you lands!
Serve the LORD with gladness;
Come before His presence with singing.
Psalm 100:1-2

I will sing of mercy and justice;
To You, O LORD, I will sing praises.
Psalm 101:1

Third Verses Only

I have been in many church services over the years in which the person leading the congregational singing announced a hymn and said: "Let's sing the first, second and last verses." Most hymns, you understand, consist of four verses.

Admittedly, I don't hear this much anymore because most congregations do not sing from a hymnal but rather from the words posted on screens. Even then third verses are oftentimes omitted.

So this question has often popped into my mind down through the years: what's wrong with the third verse? I think it's time for us to set things right. Because we've had so many services in which third verses were skipped, I propose that we have a few services in which we sing only third verses!

Why do we so often leave out the third verse? Is it because we are in a hurry to get through worship? Are we leaving the impression that this worship business is so dull and uninspiring that we want to get through it as quickly as possible so we can get back to the really important stuff, that is, our lives away from church? We never hear anyone say:

"Let's just skip the third quarter of the football game." Why? Because we are so interested in the game that we don't want it to be shortened. Why do we want to shorten worship?

The skipping of the third verse is particularly egregious when the hymn is Trinitarian, as is the case with *Come, Thou Almighty King*. The first verse addresses the Father, the second the Son, the third the Holy Spirit, and the fourth all three persons. I have actually been in services in which the third verse of that great hymn was not sung. Imagine it — singing a hymn addressing the Trinity without including the verse that addresses the Holy Spirit! And how we need to be singing to Him, the Holy Spirit, these words:

> *Come, Holy Comforter, Thy sacred witness bear,*
> *In this glad hour!*
> *Thou who almighty art, Now rule in ev'ry heart,*
> *And ne'er from us depart,*
> *Spirit of pow'r.*

One pastor of music and worship, Andrew Lucius, has pointed out how very important it is for the widow facing her first Christmas without her husband to join the congregation in singing the third verse of *Joy to the World*:

> *No more let sins and sorrows grow,*
> *Nor thorns infest the ground;*
> *He comes to make His blessings flow*
> *Far as the curse is found ...*

Lucius says of this woman: "When she's feeling the power of the curse and its application in death, I want her to be singing and believing that."

Just mark me down as a third verse guy. I never want to be in a service that sings *Jesus Paid It All* without singing:

> *For nothing good have I, Whereby Thy grace to claim;*
> *I'll wash my garments white, In the blood of Calvary's Lamb.*

And I never want to skip these words:

> *Dear dying Lamb, Thy precious blood*
> *Shall never lose its power*
> *Till all the ransomed church of God*
> *Be saved to sin no more.*

My heart yearns to sing the words of Fanny J. Crosby:

> *Trusting only in Thy merit, Would I seek Thy face;*
> *Heal my wounded, broken spirit, Save me by Thy grace.*

And please let me sing:

> *My sin—oh, the bliss of this glorious thought:*
> *My sin not in part, but the whole*
> *Is nailed to the cross and I bear it no more,*
> *Praise the Lord, praise the Lord, O my soul!*

Let's never fail to sing these words:

> *And when I think that God, His Son not sparing,*
> *Sent Him to die, I scarce can take it in,*
> *That on the cross, my burden gladly bearing,*
> *He bled and died to take away my sin.*

In these days, we need great worship, and great worship requires great thoughts regarding God. Many of those great thoughts are found in third verses. So let's sing them, and sing them from our hearts. "To Him be glory in the Church…" (Eph. 3:21).

-31-

From God's Word, the Bible...

Jesus answered and said to them, "Are you not therefore mistaken, because you do not know the Scriptures nor the power of God? For when they rise from the dead, they neither marry nor are given in marriage, but are like angels in heaven. But concerning the dead, that they rise, have you not read in the book of Moses, in the burning bush passage, how God spoke to him, saying, 'I am the God of Abraham, the God of Isaac, and the God of Jacob'? He is not the God of the dead, but the God of the living.
You are therefore greatly mistaken."

Mark 12:24-27

Sad Sadducees!

The Sadducees and the Pharisees were religious sects when Jesus was engaged in His public ministry. The Sadducees were the religious liberals of their day. One of their trademark beliefs was that there is no such thing as a bodily resurrection. The Pharisees, on the other hand, affirmed the resurrection.

One of the favorite pastimes of the Sadducees was coming up with resurrection riddles to tie the Pharisees in knots. The Pharisees and Sadducees were united in one respect—their dislike for Jesus. Their disdain for Jesus prompted the Sadducees to try one of their riddles on Him.

This riddle had to do with a particular provision in the Law of Moses. If a man married a woman and died without children, she would become the wife of his brother. In this particular riddle, a man married a woman and died without children. She then became the wife of the brother next to him in age. This brother also died, so the woman became the wife of the next oldest brother, and so it went until she was the wife of seven brothers in sequence. After the seventh brother died, the woman also died.

The thing the Sadducees wanted to know was whose wife she would be if there should in fact be a resurrection from the dead. The thing I'd like to know is this: what was there about this woman that caused every man she married to die? But I digress.

These smug Sadducees were secure in their belief that they had put Jesus into a dilemma from which He could not extricate Himself. However, they soon discovered that they were wrong. Jesus was equal to the occasion. He told the Sadducees that they were woefully ignorant of "the Scriptures" and "the power of God" (v. 24).

The Sadducees had a very small Bible, regarding only the writings of Moses (the first five books of the Old Testament) as being authoritative. But Jesus showed them that even their small Bible affirmed the resurrection of the body. When the Lord appeared to Moses in the burning bush, He declared Himself to be the God of Abraham, Isaac, and Jacob (Exod. 3:1-6). He didn't say He "was" their God. He rather said: "I am" their God. That meant that the souls of Abraham, Isaac, and Jacob were alive and well, and the fact that their souls were alive was proof of the resurrection of their bodies. God made us body and soul—one entity—and one part can't have eternal life without the other!

The Sadducees also had a very small God. They seemed to think the resurrection of the body was too much for God. Their resurrection riddle about the woman with seven husbands assumed that if there is a resurrection of the body it will mean a continuation of life as we have known it here. The point they missed is that God is powerful enough to not only raise the body but also to create a whole new way of living in which the problems of this life will no longer be problems.

There are still many resurrection skeptics with their own

resurrection riddles. They point to soldiers who were blown to bits in war and ask how there could be a resurrection for such. They point to those who have been dead for so long that their bodies have completely decomposed, and they rule out the possibility of a resurrection. The point they conveniently ignore is the power of God. If God was powerful enough to make Adam from the dust (Gen. 2:7), He is powerful enough to raise a person from the dust.

Their small Bible and their small God caused the Sadducees to be "greatly mistaken" (v. 27). And their great mistakes robbed them of the joyful confidence that God's people will live as bodies and souls in eternal glory. Their mistakes made them sad Sadducees.

Let's make it our business to be sure that we don't keep company with the sad Sadducees. Let's believe in the Word of God and in the power of God, and let's rejoice in the glorious future that the Word of God promises and the power of God guarantees.

God has promised a wonderful future in eternity to everyone who turns away from sin and trusts in His Son, the Lord Jesus Christ, and who lives a life in union with Him. You can be assured of sins forgiven in this life through the saving work of Jesus, and you can look forward to a glorious resurrected life in a perfect body in the new heavens and the new earth.

About the Author

Roger Ellsworth is a retired pastor, active in ministry and writing, who lives in Jackson, Tennessee. He and his wife, Sylvia, love the message of the Bible, and they enjoy sharing the wonderful counsel of the Word of God in language that ordinary people can understand and appreciate.

Roger has written numerous books on the Christian faith, and has exercised a preaching ministry for over fifty years. His sermons are available to listen for free on SermonAudio.com.

The Series

Enjoy collecting the My Coffee Cup Meditations Series.

The "Thumbs-Up" Man 978-0-9988812-5-6 (Series#1)
A Dog and A Clock 978-0-9988812-9-4 (Series#2)
When God Blocks Our Path 978-0-9988812-4-9 (Series#3)
Fading Lines, Unfading Hope 978-0-9996559-1-7 (Series#4)
The Day the Milk Spilled 978-0-9965168-6-0 (Series#5)
"Where Are the Donuts?" 978-0-9965168-7-7 (Series#6)

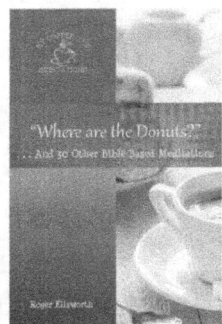

www.mycoffeecupmeditations.com

www.ingramcontent.com/pod-product-compliance
Lightning Source LLC
Chambersburg PA
CBHW070613010526
44118CB00012B/1503